Math in FOCUS®
Singapore Math
by Marshall Cavendish

Extra Practice

Author
Meena Newaskar

mc Marshall Cavendish
Education

US Distributor

HOUGHTON MIFFLIN HARCOURT

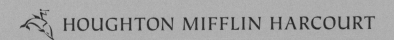

COMMON CORE

© Copyright 2009, 2013 Edition Marshall Cavendish International (Singapore) Private Limited

Published by Marshall Cavendish Education
An imprint of Marshall Cavendish International (Singapore) Private Limited
Times Centre, 1 New Industrial Road, Singapore 536196
Customer Service Hotline: (65) 6411 0820
E-mail: tmesales@sg.marshallcavendish.com
Website: www.marshallcavendish.com/education

Distributed by
Houghton Mifflin Harcourt
222 Berkeley Street
Boston, MA 02116
Tel: 617-351-5000
Website: www.hmheducation.com/mathinfocus

First published 2009
2013 Edition

Math in Focus® Extra Practice 1A
ISBN 978-0-669-01567-6

Printed in Singapore

2 3 4 5 6 7 8   1897   18 17 16 15 14 13
4500371013   A B C D E

Contents

CHAPTER 4

Subtraction Facts to 10

CHAPTER 5

Shapes and Patterns

Length

Introducing

Math in Focus®

Extra Practice

Extra Practice 1A and *1B*, written to complement *Math in Focus®: Singapore Math by Marshall Cavendish* Grade 1, offer further practice very similar to the Practice exercises in the Student Books and Workbooks for on-level students.

Extra Practice provides ample questions to reinforce all the concepts taught, and includes challenging questions in the Put on Your Thinking Cap! pages. These pages provide extra non-routine problem-solving opportunities, strengthening critical thinking skills.

Extra Practice is an excellent option for homework, or may be used in class or after school. It is intended for students who simply need more practice to become confident, or secure students who are aiming for excellence.

BLANK

Name: _____ **Date:** _____

CHAPTER 1 Numbers to 10

Lesson 1 Counting to 10

Count.
Write the numbers.

1.  _____

2.  _____

Color.

3. 9 flowers

4. five stars

Count.
Circle the correct word.

5.

five   four   three

6.

eight   six   nine

7.

four   six   five

Match.

8.   7   3   5   8

●   ●   ●   ●

●   ●   ●   ●

eight   five   three   seven

Count.
Write the numbers.

9.   There are _____ coconut trees.

10.   There are _____ houses.

11.   There are _____ birds.

12.   There are _____ coconuts.

13.   I can see _____ sun.

Name: ______________________ Date: ______________

Count.
Write the numbers in words.

one	two	four

14. There are ______________ .

15. There are ______________ .

16. There is ______________ .

17. There are ______________ .

18.   How old is Jason?

He is _____ years old.

Complete each number pattern.

19.   0, _____, 2, _____, 4, 5

20.   10, _____, _____, 7, 6

21.   5, _____, 7, 8, _____, 10

22.   6, 5, _____, _____, 2

Count.
Circle the correct word.

23.

🦆	two	one	four	six
🦘	three	six	four	five
🦒	five	seven	nine	six
🐻	one	three	two	ten

Lesson 2   Comparing Numbers

Match.
Then circle the correct answer.

people

igloos

1.   There are more (people / igloos) than (people / igloos).

birds

eggs

2.   There are (more / fewer) birds than eggs.

3.   There are (more / fewer) eggs than birds.

Look at the picture.
Count the things.

Fill in the blanks.
Circle the one that is more.

4.

balloons _____   party hats _____

Fill in the blanks.
Circle the one that is fewer.

5.

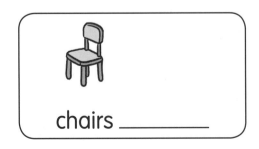 

chairs _____   table _____

● **Fill in the blanks.**
Circle the ones that have the same number.

6. 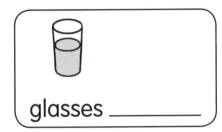 glasses _____    candles _____

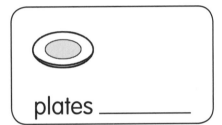 plates _____

● **Count.**

7. Color the two trees that have the same number of apples.

8. How many trees have 4 apples each? _____

Count the number of legs.
Circle the animals that have the same number of legs.

9.

10.

11.

12.

● **Color the T-shirt that shows the number that is less.**

13.

14.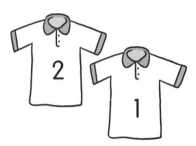

15.

16.

● **Color the jellyfish that shows the greater number.**

17.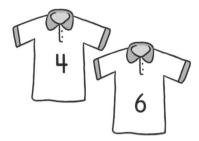

18.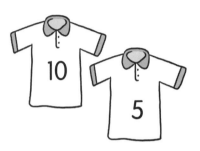

19.

20.

Color the numbers that are greater than 2 but less than 6.

21.

Check (✓) the group that has more.

22.

23.

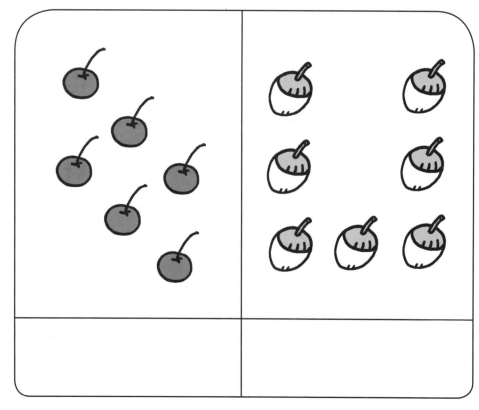

Check (✓) the group that has fewer.

24.

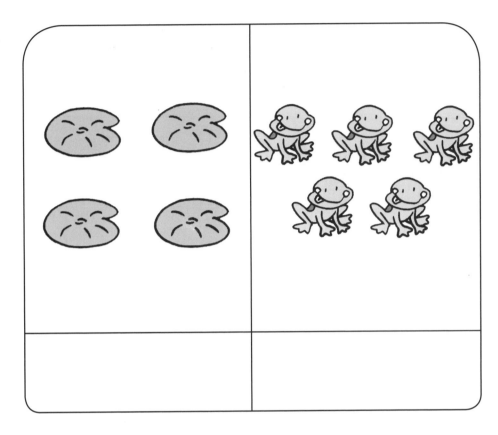

25.

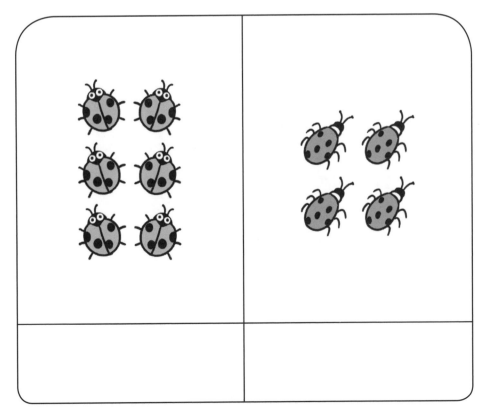

Name: _____   **Date:** _____

Circle the groups that show the same number.

26.

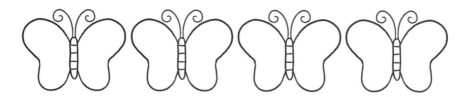

27.

Lesson 3   Making Number Patterns
Circle.

1.   Which nest has more than 7 eggs?

2.   Which boy has 1 fewer than 6 balls?

3.   Which basket has 1 more than 3 fruits?

Match.
Then circle the correct answer.

bird

nest

4.   There is 1 more (bird / nest) than (bird / nest).

caterpillar

leaf

5.   There is 1 less (caterpillar / leaf) than (caterpillar / leaf).

Name: _____   **Date:** _____

Count the worms.
Write the number in each box.

Chicks A, B, C, and D eat some worms.

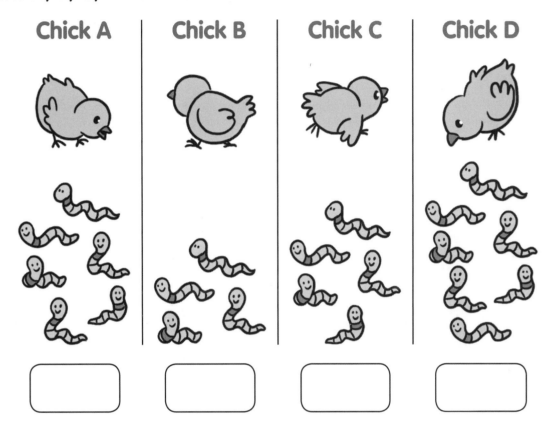

| Chick A | Chick B | Chick C | Chick D |

6.   Chick _____ eats 1 worm more than Chick B.

7.   Chick _____ eats 1 worm fewer than Chick D.

8.   Chick _____ eats the most worms.

Complete each number pattern.

9. 6, 5, 4, 3, _____, _____

10. 8, 7, _____, _____, 4, 3

11. 0, 1, _____, 3, _____

12. 5, _____, 7, _____, 9, 10

13. 8, _____, _____, 5, 4

Fill in the blanks.

14. 1 more than 7 is _____.

15. 1 less than 8 is _____.

16. 1 more than _____ is 10.

17. 5 is 1 less than _____.

18. _____ is 1 more than 4.

19. _____ is 1 less than 10.

20. _____ is 1 more than 0.

 **Put on Your Thinking Cap!**

The picture shows a group of frogs that have spots.

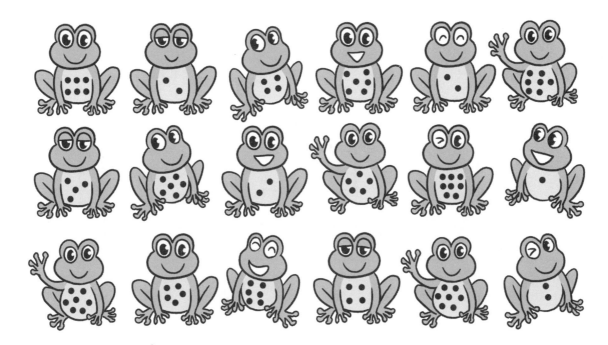

1. Cross out the frogs that have more than 5 spots.

2. Circle the frogs that have fewer than 4 spots.

Draw the correct number of bones in each plate.

3. There are 5 bones.
Jake has 1 more bone than Ginger.
How many bones does each dog have?

2 Number Bonds

Lesson 1 Making Number Bonds (Part 1)

Look at the picture.
Complete the number bond.

1.

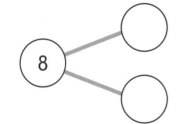

Look at the ▣.
Fill in the parts.

2.

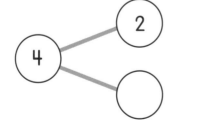

3.

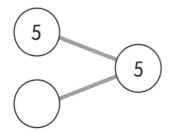

4.

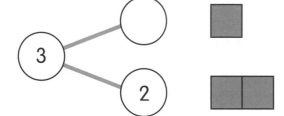

5.

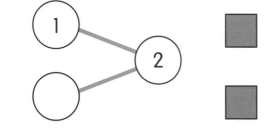

6.

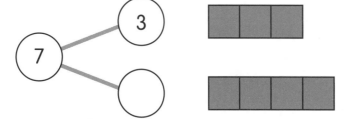

7.

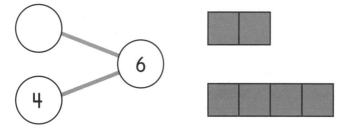

8.

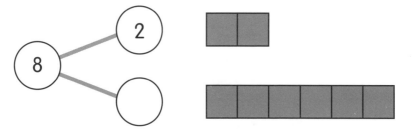

● **Complete the number bonds.**

9.

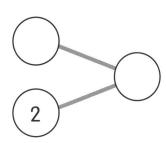

10.

11. I put 8 marbles into three cups.
There are 3 marbles in one cup.

There are _____ and _____ marbles in the other cups.

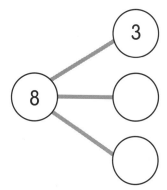

12. Show two ways to make 7.

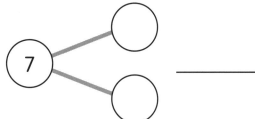

_____ and _____ make 7.

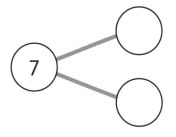

_____ and _____ make 7.

13. Show three ways to make 6.

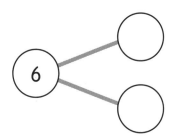

_____ and _____ make 6.

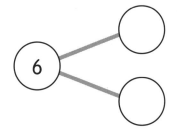

_____ and _____ make 6.

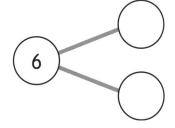

_____ and _____ make 6.

Lesson 1   Making Number Bonds (Part 2)

Circle the two numbers that make the number in the .

1.	8	5	2	3
2.	6	0	7	1
3.	5	3	2	4
4.	3	5	0	6

10

8

9

6

Match to make 9.

5.   4 •   • 2

3 •   • 5

7 •   • 6

Match to make 10.

6.   8 •   • 1

9 •   • 2

3 •   • 7

Fill in the parts.

7. Show ways to make 7.

Fill in the blanks.

8. 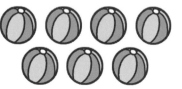 $+$ $= ?$

4 and 3 make _____.

9.  $+ ? =$ (balls)

7 and _____ make 9.

Lesson 1   Making Number Bonds (Part 3)

Count.
Fill in the blanks.

1.   3 and 2 make _____.

2.   _____ and _____ make 4.

3.   3 and 4 make _____.

4.   _____ and _____ make 3.

Use two colors.

Color the ☐ to show the parts that make the whole.

Fill in the blanks.

5.   6 and _____ make 9.

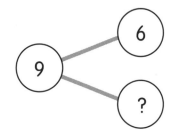

6.   8 and 0 make _____.

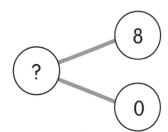

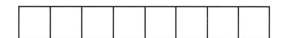

● **Circle the objects to show the parts.**

7.

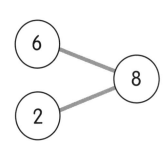

8.

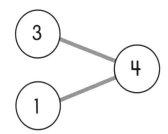

Look at the pictures.
Complete the number bonds.

9.

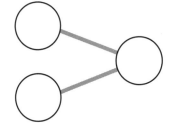

10.

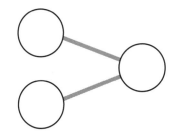

Look at the pictures.
Complete the number bonds.

11.

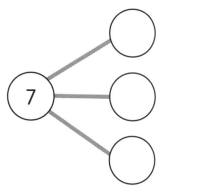

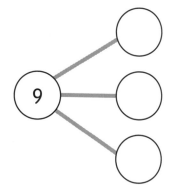

12.

13.

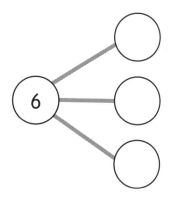

Put on Your Thinking Cap!

1. Little Bo Bo, the shepherd, has lost his sheep.
   He had 9 sheep.
   He can only find 2 sheep now.

Find and color the missing sheep.

How many sheep are missing? _____
Then complete the number bond.

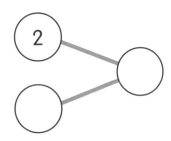

2. Brian and Eddy are wearing T-shirts with numbers on them.
Match each bag and cap to the right boy.

CHAPTER 3 Addition Facts to 10

Lesson 1   Ways to Add (Part 1)

Look at the pictures.
Fill in the blanks.

1.

$$4 + _____ = _____$$

2.

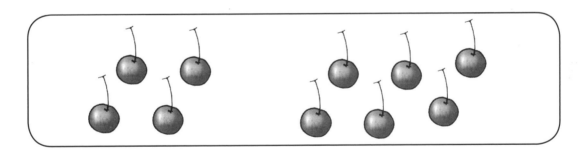

$$_____ + 6 = _____$$

3.

$$_____ + _____ = _____$$

Add.
Count on from the greater number.

4.   6 + 3 = _____   5.   2 + 7 = _____

6.   8 + 2 = _____   7.   4 + 5 = _____

8.   3 + 5 = _____   9.   3 + 4 = _____

Add.
Then circle the answer that is 2 more than 8.

10.   **5 + 2   6 + 4   7 + 1   8 + 0**

_____   _____   _____   _____

Fill in the blanks.

11.   2 more than 5 is _____.

12.   _____ is 3 more than 7.

13.   1 more than _____ is 6.

14.   2 more than _____ is 9.

Lesson 1   Ways to Add (Part 2)
Complete the number bonds.
Then fill in the blanks.

1.

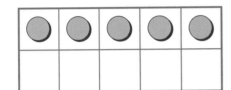 

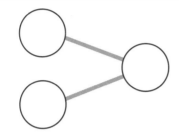

$5 + 1 =$ _____

2.

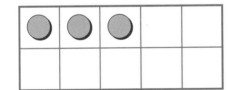 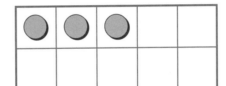

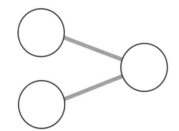

$3 +$ _____ $=$ _____

3.

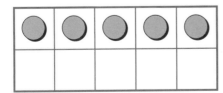 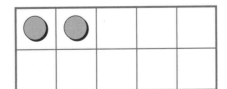

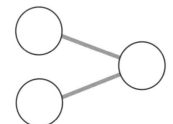

_____ $+$ _____ $=$ _____

Look at the pictures.
Complete the number bonds.
Then fill in the blanks.

4.

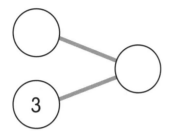

_____ + 3 = _____

5.

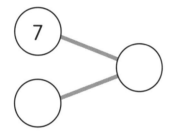

7 + _____ = _____

6.

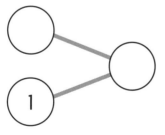

_____ + 1 = _____

Complete the number bonds.
Then fill in the blanks.

7.   6 + 3 = _____

   3 + 6 = _____

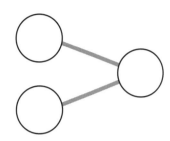

8.   2 + 5 = _____

   5 + 2 = _____

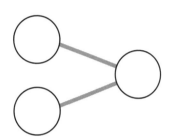

9.   3 + _____ = 7

   _____ + 3 = 7

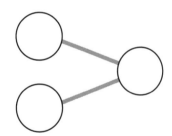

10.   _____ + 8 = 8

   8 + _____ = 8

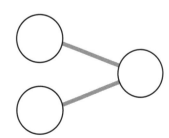

11.   4 + _____ = 6

   _____ + 4 = 6

12. Add.
Then match each key to a lock.

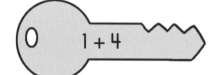

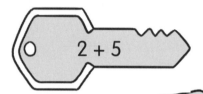

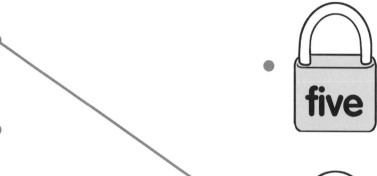

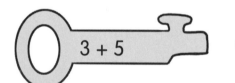

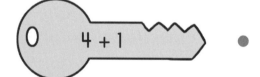

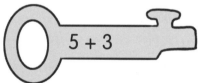

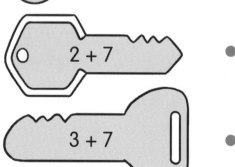

Lesson 2 Making Addition Stories

Look at the picture.

Complete the addition story.

1. _____ birds are flying.

    _____ birds are not flying.

    _____ + _____ = _____

    _____ birds are at the beach in all.

Write an addition story about the turtles in the picture.

2.

swimming
beach
crawling

Look at the picture.
Write an addition story.

3.

Fill in the numbers on the steps.
Then fill in the blanks.

4. Bob is climbing up the stairs.
He starts on Step 1.
He climbs up two steps and lands on Step _____.

5. Bob starts on Step 5.
He climbs up two steps and lands on Step _____.
He climbs up two more steps.

Now he is on Step _____.

Lesson 3   Real-World Problems: Addition

Solve.

1.

The tree has 6 apples.
The basket contains 3 apples.

☐ ◯ ☐ ◯ ☐

There are _____ apples in all.

2.

_____ children are playing basketball.

_____ children are watching the game.

☐ ◯ ☐ ◯ ☐

_____ children are at the game in all.

3.

_____ children are on the .

_____ children are on the .

_____ children are at the playground in all.

4.

_____ turtles are on the .

_____ turtles are in the .

There are _____ turtles in all.

Put on Your Thinking Cap!

1.

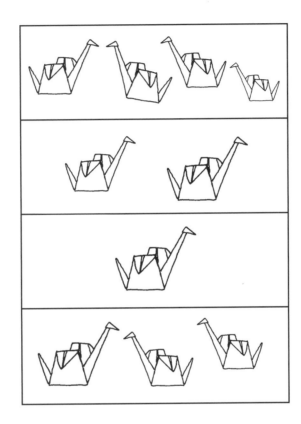

Ben and his friends make 10 paper cranes.

• The cranes are made of red, yellow, blue, and green paper.

• Red is used more than other colors.

• There are more blue cranes than green cranes.

• Only one crane is yellow.

Color each row of cranes red, yellow, blue, or green to match the description.

2. Write the numbers 1, 2, 3, 4, and 5 in the correct circles.
Make the three circles on each line add up to 9.

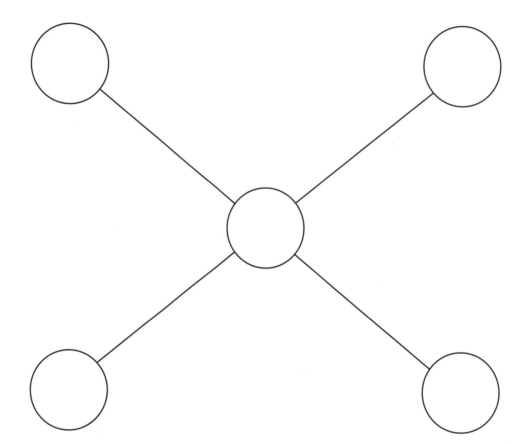

Subtraction Facts to 10

Lesson 1   Ways to Subtract (Part 1)

Fill in the blanks.

1.   Cross out 2 .

There are _____  left.

2.   Cross out 1 .

There are _____ left.

3.   Cross out 3 .

There is _____ left.

Take away to subtract.
Then complete the subtraction sentence.

4.

$8 - 5 =$ _____

5.

$7 - 2 =$ _____

6.

$7 - 6 =$ _____

7.

$9 -$ _____ $= 6$

8.

$8 -$ _____ $= 6$

Cross out to subtract.

9. ◯◯◯◯◯◯◯◯◯◯

$10 - 5 =$ _____

10. ☐☐☐☐☐☐☐

$7 - 0 =$ _____

11. △△△△△△△△△

$9 - 5 =$ _____

Cross out to subtract.

12.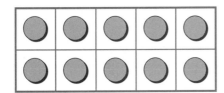

$10 - 2 =$ _____

13.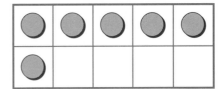

$6 - 1 =$ _____

14.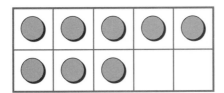

$8 - 3 =$ _____

15.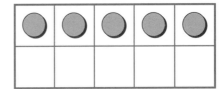

$5 - 4 =$ _____

Subtract.
Count on from the number that is less.
Then fill in the blanks.

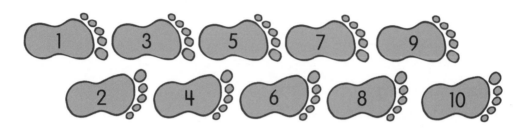

16.   5 – 3 = _____   **17.**   6 – 4 = _____

18.   7 – 2 = _____   **19.**   10 – 4 = _____

Solve.

20. _____ is 1 less than 3.

21. _____ is 1 less than 8.

22. _____ is 1 less than 5.

Count back from the greater number to subtract.

23.   9 – 5 = _____ | 1 | 2 | 3 | 4 | 5 | 6 | 7 | 8 | 9 |

24.   6 – 0 = _____ | 1 | 2 | 3 | 4 | 5 | 6 |

25.   5 – 4 = _____ | 1 | 2 | 3 | 4 | 5 |

26.   7 – 5 = _____ | 1 | 2 | 3 | 4 | 5 | 6 | 7 |

Lesson 1   Ways to Subtract (Part 2)

Fill in the number bonds.
Complete the subtraction sentences.

1.

$6 - 2 =$ _____

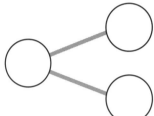

2.

$8 - 3 =$ _____

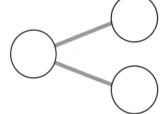

3.

$9 - 5 =$ _____

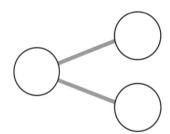

4.

$7 - 6 =$ _____

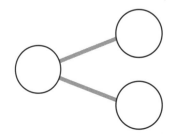

Match.

5. $8 - 1 =$ _____    ●   ●

6. $10 - 5 =$ _____    ●   ●

7. $6 - 0 =$ _____    ●   ●

8. $9 - 6 =$ _____    ●   ●   6

9. $10 - 6 =$ _____    ●   ●   4

10. $4 - 4 =$ _____    ●   ●   3

Fill in the blanks.

Fred the frog is hopping back on the path.
Where does he land each time?

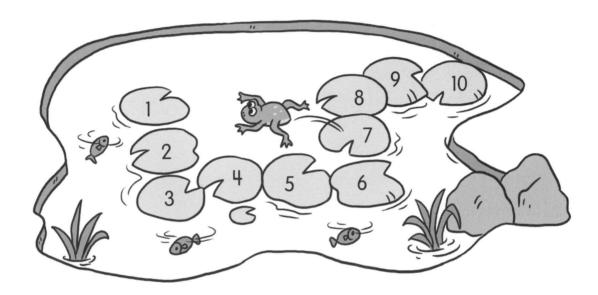

11. Fred starts at 10.
He hops 2 steps back.

He lands on _____.

12. Fred starts at 8.
He hops 3 steps back.

He lands on _____.

13. Fred starts at 9.
He hops 5 steps back.

He lands on _____.

14. Fred starts at 7.
He hops 4 steps back.

He lands on _____.

Fill in the number bonds.
Complete the subtraction sentences.

15.   How many trees are small?

 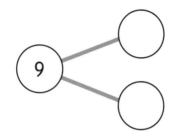

9 – _____ = _____

_____ trees are small.

16.   How many birds do not fly away?

_____ – 3 = _____

_____ birds do not fly away.

Lesson 2   Making Subtraction Stories

Look at the pictures.
Fill in the number bonds.
Complete the subtraction stories.

1.

There are 7 carrots.

The bunny eats _____ carrots.

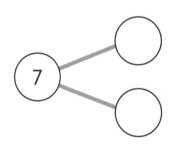

7 – _____ = _____

_____ carrots are left.

2.

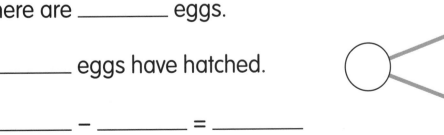

There are _____ eggs.

_____ eggs have hatched.

_____ – _____ = _____

_____ egg has not hatched.

3.

There are _____ slices of pizza.

The children eat _____ slices.

_____ slices of pizza are left.

4.

There are _____ children.

_____ are girls.

_____ are boys.

Lesson 3   Real-World Problems: Subtraction

Solve.

Write the subtraction sentences.

1. There are 9 penguins.
    3 are swimming.
    How many penguins are not swimming?

_____ penguins are not swimming.

2. A monkey has 7 bananas.
He eats 3 bananas.
How many bananas are left?

```
┌──────┐   ┌──────┐     ┌──────┐
│      │ ◯ │      │  =  │      │
└──────┘   └──────┘     └──────┘
```

_____ bananas are left.

3. Nora finds 6 seashells.
Only 1 is big.
The rest are small.
How many seashells are small?

```
┌──────┐   ┌──────┐     ┌──────┐
│      │ ◯ │      │  =  │      │
└──────┘   └──────┘     └──────┘
```

_____ seashells are small.

4. A nest has 8 chicks.
3 chicks run away.
How many chicks are left in the nest?

_____ chicks are left in the nest.

5. Glen has 5 fish.
3 are small fish.
The rest are big fish.
How many are big fish?

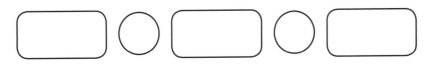

_____ are big fish.

6.   Bobo has 9 balloons.
He burst 2 balloons.
How many balloons are left?

_____ balloons are left.

7.   Lucy has 7 strawberries.
She gives 2 strawberries to her sister.
How many strawberries does she have left?

She has _____ strawberries left.

Lesson 4   Making Fact Families

Make a fact family for each picture.

1.

_____ + _____ = _____

_____ + _____ = _____

_____ − _____ = _____

_____ − _____ = _____

2.

_____ + _____ = _____

_____ + _____ = _____

_____ − _____ = _____

_____ − _____ = _____

Solve.

3.   Helen has some dolls.
She puts party hats on 3 of her dolls.
4 dolls do not have hats.
How many dolls does she have?

_____ – 3 = 4

3 + 4 = _____ is the
related addition fact.

She has _____ dolls.

4.   There are 2 turtles on the grass.
Some turtles are in the pond.
John counts 6 turtles altogether.
How many turtles are in the pond?

2 + _____ = 6

6 – 2 = _____ is the
related subtraction fact.

_____ turtles are in the pond.

Put on Your Thinking Cap!

Samantha has four activities this month.
The dates of those activities are circled on her calendar.
What is the date of each activity?

Sunday	Monday	Tuesday	Wednesday	Thursday	Friday	Saturday
	1	2	3	④	5	⑥
7	⑧	9	⑩	11	12	13
14	15	16	17	18	19	20
21	22	23	24	25	26	27
28	29	30				

1. Amy's birthday party will be on a Saturday.

    Date: _____

2. The school play will be on a Monday.

    Date: _____

3. Her class trip to the zoo is 2 days before the birthday party.

    Date: _____

4. Music practice starts 2 days after the school play.

    Date: _____

5.   Peter has 4 pets.

Each pet is a or a .

The animals have a total of 10 legs.

How many  and how many does he have?

Does he have 2 and 2 ? Guess and check to find the answer.

He has _____ and _____ .

Name: _____   **Date:** _____

Test Prep

80

for Chapters 1 to 4

Multiple Choice (10 × 2 points = 20 points)

Fill in the circle next to the correct answer.

1. There are _____ goldfish in the tank.

(A) 1   (B) 3   (C) 4   (D) 5

2. There are _____ crabs.

(A) four   (B) five   (C) six   (D) seven

3. Which set makes 10?

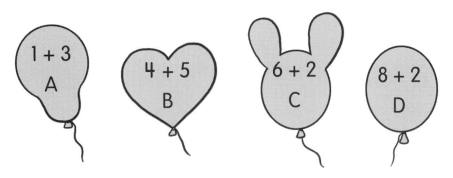

(A) A   (B) B   (C) C   (D) D

4. _____ + 2 = 5.

(A) 1   (B) 3   (C) 6   (D) 7

5. 8 – _____ = 1.

(A) 4   (B) 6   (C) 7   (D) 8

6. I had 9 marbles.
I gave some to Leo.
I have 7 marbles now.

I gave Leo _____ marbles.

(A) 1   (B) 2   (C) 3   (D) 6

7. Which pair of numbers makes 10?

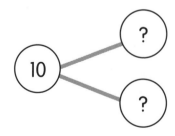

(A) 8, 2   (B) 7, 1   (C) 5, 4   (D) 6, 2

8. Look at the picture.
Which addition or subtraction sentence
does <u>not</u> match the picture?

Ⓐ 5 + 2 = 7

Ⓑ 6 + 1 = 7

Ⓒ 7 − 2 = 5

Ⓓ 7 − 5 = 2

9. Jim has 4 balloons.
Ben gives him 2 more balloons.

Jim has _____ balloons now.

Ⓐ 4   Ⓑ 5   Ⓒ 6   Ⓓ 8

10. There are 8 birds.
4 birds are resting.
How many birds are flying?

Ⓐ 4   Ⓑ 6   Ⓒ 8   Ⓓ 10

Short Answer

Match. (4 points)

11. Are there more rabbits or carrots?

rabbits

carrots

There are more _____ than

_____.

Write + or – in each circle. (2 × 2 points = 4 points)

12. 7 ◯ 2 = 5

13. 5 ◯ 1 = 6

Match. (4 × 2 points = 8 points)

14.
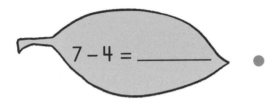
7 – 4 = _____

15.
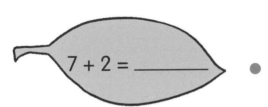
8 – 3 = _____

16.
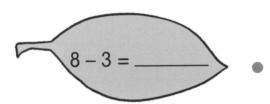
7 + 2 = _____

17.
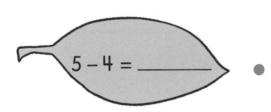
5 – 4 = _____

5

3

1

9

Fill in the blanks. (4 × 1 point = 4 points)

18.   2 and _____ make 10.

19.   1 more than 8 is _____.

20.   2 less than 3 is _____.

21.   _____ is 2 more than 0.

Color the set that have answers that are
2 less than 10. (4 points)

22.

| 7 + 3 | 4 + 4 | 6 + 1 | 5 + 3 |

Look at the picture.
Fill in the number bond.
Then write the subtraction sentence. (6 points)

23.

⬜ − ⬜ = ⬜

Name: _____   **Date:** _____

Fill in the number bond.
Write a fact family for the picture. (4 × 2 points = 8 points)

  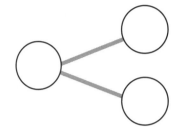

24. [   ] + [   ] = [   ]

25. [   ] + [   ] = [   ]

26. [   ] − [   ] = [   ]

27. [   ] − [   ] = [   ]

Complete each number sentence. (5 × 2 points = 10 points)

28. 8 + 2 = _____ | 1 | 2 | 3 | 4 | 5 | 6 | 7 | 8 | 9 | 10 |

29. 8 − _____ = 8 | 1 | 2 | 3 | 4 | 5 | 6 | 7 | 8 |

30. 7 − _____ = 4 | 1 | 2 | 3 | 4 | 5 | 6 | 7 |

31. 6 + _____ = 9 | 1 | 2 | 3 | 4 | 5 | 6 | 7 | 8 | 9 |

32. _____ − 3 = 5 | 1 | 2 | 3 | 4 | 5 | 6 | 7 | 8 |

Extended Response (2 × 6 points = 12 points)

Solve.
Show your work.
Write the number sentence.

33.   There are 6 red balloons.
There are 2 yellow balloons.
How many balloons are there in all?

There are _____ balloons in all.

34.   There are 10 pencils.
There are 4 fewer pens.
How many pens are there?

There are _____ pens.

CHAPTER  5 Shapes and Patterns

Lesson 1   Exploring Plane Shapes (Part 1)

Name the shapes.

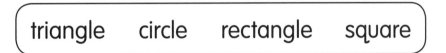

triangle   circle   rectangle   square

1.

_____

2.

_____

3.

_____

4.

_____

Color the squares.

5.

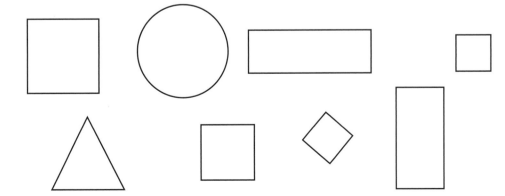

Color the shapes that are <u>not</u> rectangles.

6.

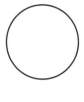
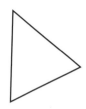

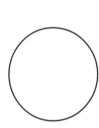
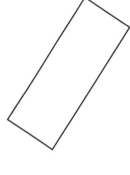

Which shape is missing?
Color the name.

7.

| square |
| triangle |
| circle |
| rectangle |

● **What shape can you make using <u>all</u> the pieces?**

8.

I can make a _____.

Color the bigger square.

9.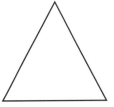

● **Color the smaller circle.**

10.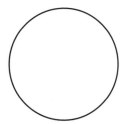

●

Circle the smallest triangle.

11.

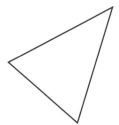 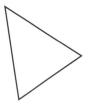 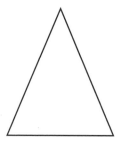

Circle the biggest rectangle.

12.

Draw a smaller triangle.

13.

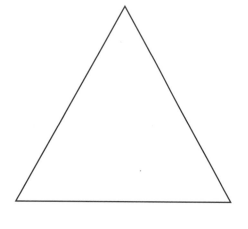 

Lesson 1   Exploring Plane Shapes (Part 2)

Which shapes are the same?
Color them.

1.   Color the squares red.

2.   Color the circles blue.

3.   Color the rectangles green.

4.   Color the triangles yellow.

Read.
Then draw and name the shape.

```
circle     triangle     square     rectangle
```

5. I have 3 sides and 3 corners.
What shape am I?

I am a _____.

6. I am a shape with no corners.
What shape am I?

I am a _____.

7. I have 4 sides and 4 corners.
What shape am I?

I am a _____.

Lesson 2   Exploring Solid Shapes

Match.

1.   cylinder   •   •

2.   sphere   •   •

3.   cube   •   •

4.   pyramid   •   •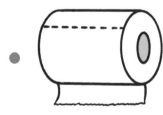

5.   rectangular prism •   •

6.   cone   •   •

Match each solid to its box.

7. Lisa needs to put the solids into the correct box.

Fill in the blanks with *stack*, *slide,* or *roll* to show the action.

8.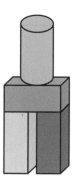

9.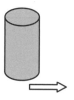

10.

_____   _____   _____

Lesson 3   Making Pictures and Models with Shapes (Part 1)

Look at the picture.
Count the shapes.
Fill in the blanks.

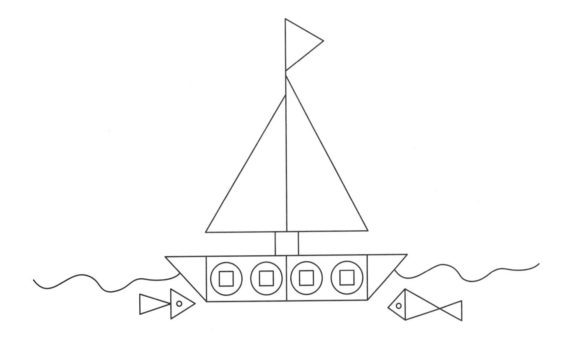

1.   I see _____ triangles.

2.   I see _____ circles.

3.   I see _____ squares.

4.   I see _____ rectangles.

Look at the picture.

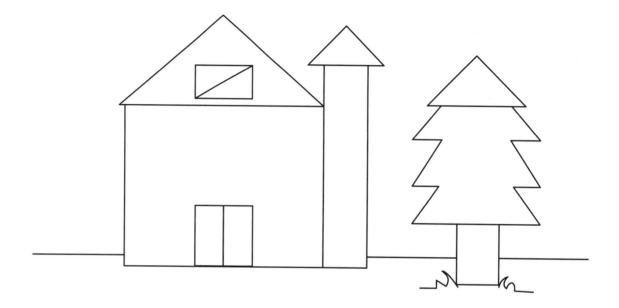

5.   Color the triangles green.

6.   How many triangles are there? _____

7.   Color the rectangles blue.

8.   How many rectangles are there? _____

Count the solid shapes.
Write the number.

9.

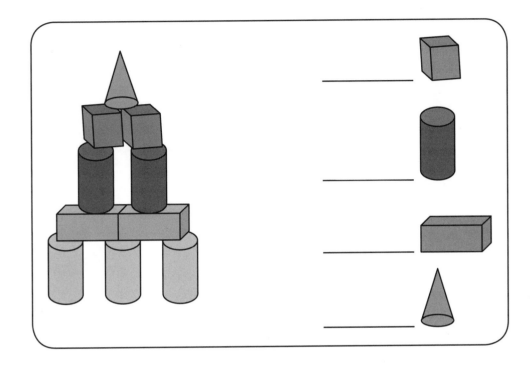

10.

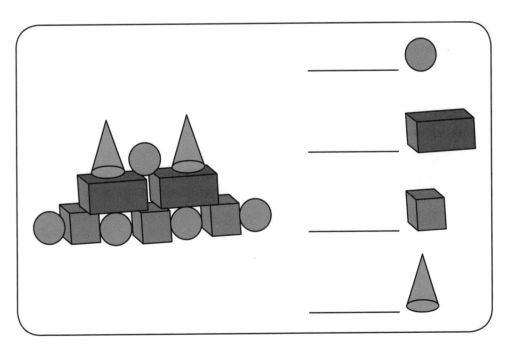

Look at the shape.
Draw a line to the same shape in the clock.

11. 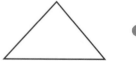 •

12. 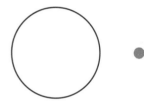 •

13. 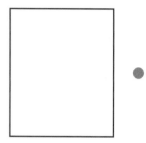 •

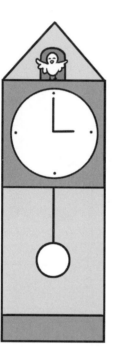

14. •

Lesson 3   Making Pictures and Models with Shapes (Part 2)

The square is made up of 7 shapes.
Look for the shapes in the square.
Write the letter in each shape.

1.

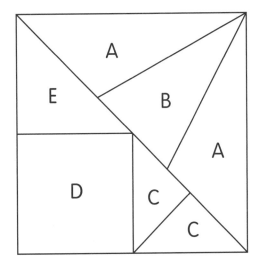

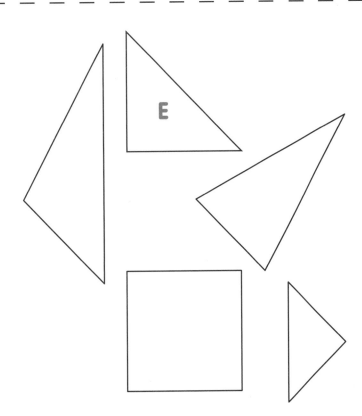

Draw a picture using triangles, squares, circles, and rectangles.

2.

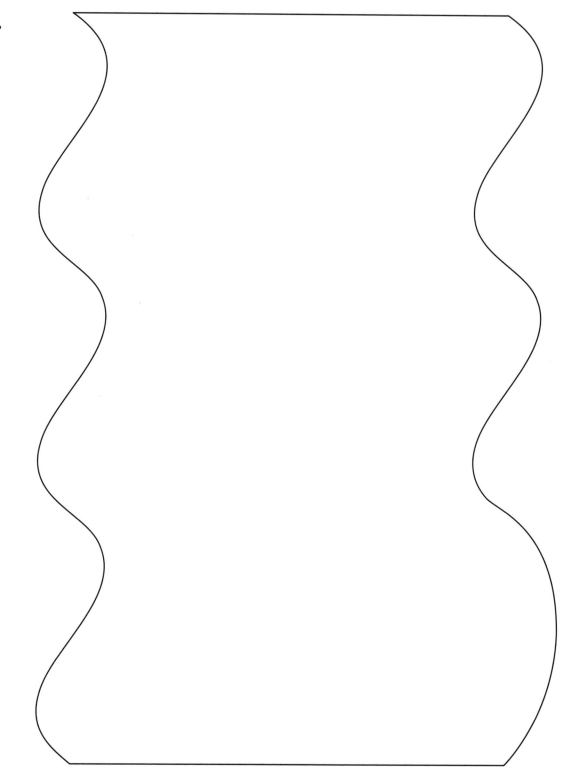

Lesson 4 Seeing Shapes Around Us

Name the shapes that are shaded.

| circle   rectangle   triangle   square |

1.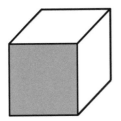

_____

2.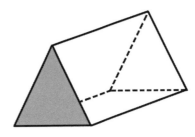

_____

3.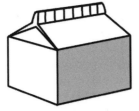

_____

4.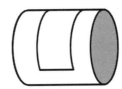

_____

5.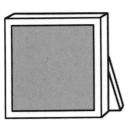

_____

6.

_____

Circle the one that does <u>not</u> belong.

7.

8.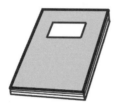

9.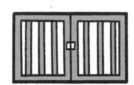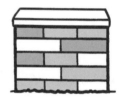

10.

11.

Lesson 5 Making Patterns with Plane Shapes

Complete the patterns.
Circle the shape that comes next.

1.

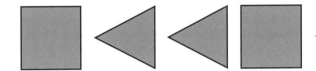

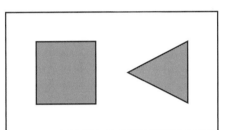

2.

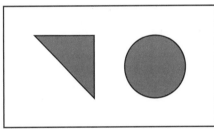

3.

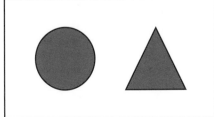

Make your own patterns.

4.

5.

6.

Lesson 6   Making Patterns with Solid Shapes

Complete the patterns.
Circle the shape that comes next.

1.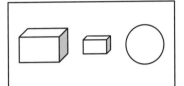

2.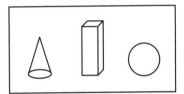

3.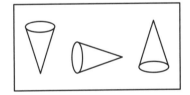

4.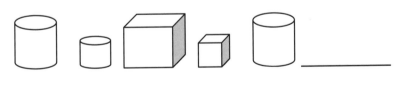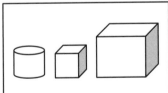

Name: _____   Date: _____

 Put on Your Thinking Cap!

Ally, Bob, Carl, and Dana each have a set of shapes.

• Bob has no triangles.

• The number of rectangles Dana has is the same as
the number of triangles Carl has.

Write the name that matches each set on the line.

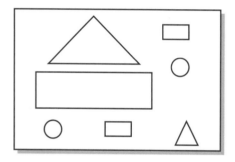

_____

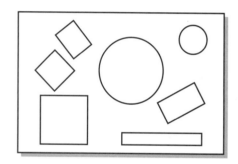

_____

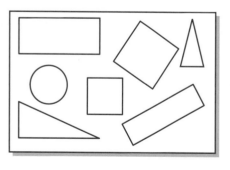

_____

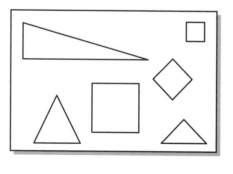

_____

Ordinal Numbers and Position

CHAPTER 6

Lesson 1   Ordinal Numbers

Cross out.

1.   the 3rd flower

1st

2.   the 5th bird

1st

3.   the 9th strawberry

1st

Draw two apples on the 8th tree.

4.

1st

Read the word.
Circle the animal.

5.   second

1st

6.   eighth

2nd

7.   first

3rd

Match.
One has been done for you.

8.

first   ●

●   second

fourth   ●

●   seventh

third   ●

●   ninth

sixth   ●

●   fifth

tenth   ●

●   eighth

Look at the picture.
Fill in the blanks.

The lizards are climbing the wall.

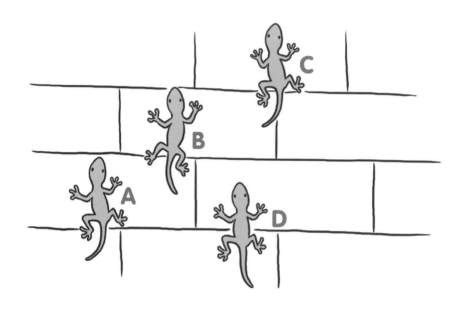

9. Which lizard is first? Lizard _____

10. Which lizard is last? Lizard _____

11. If the lizards turn around to come down, which lizard will
     be first? Lizard _____

Lesson 2   Position Words (Part 1)
Cross out.

1. the 3rd turtle from the left

Left   Right

2. the 8th seashell from the right

Left   Right

3. the 2nd crab from the right

Left   Right

4. the 5th fish from the left

Left   Right

Look at the picture.
Fill in the blanks.

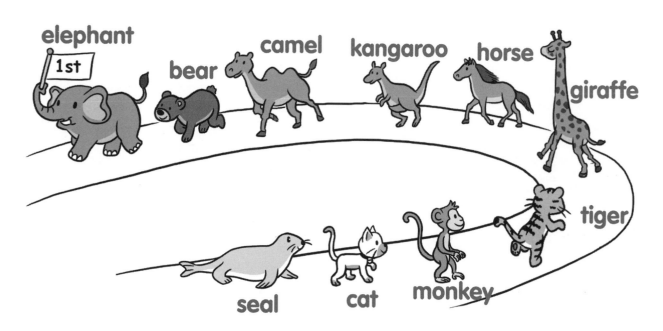

5. How many animals are marching? _____

6. Which animal is 5th? _____

7. Which animal is last? _____

8. The camel is _____.

9. The tiger is _____.

10. Which animal is before the giraffe? _____

11. Which animal is after the monkey? _____

12. The _____ is after the kangaroo.

13. The _____ is first.

14. The _____ is between the bear and the kangaroo.

15. The _____ is between the monkey and the giraffe.

16. Which animal is this?
- It is somewhere between the giraffe and the seal.
- It is <u>not</u> ninth.
- It does <u>not</u> have stripes on its body.

This animal is the _____.

Look at the picture.

Fill in the blanks with the words in the box.

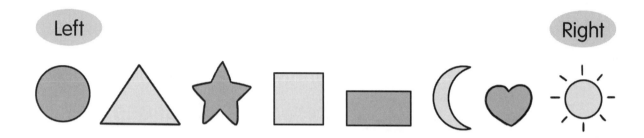

triangle   last   first   square   third

17. The star is _____ from the left.

18. The sun is _____ on the right.

19. The _____ is next to the circle.

20. The _____ is between the star and the rectangle.

21. The circle is _____ from the right.

Lesson 2 Position Words (Part 2)

Look at the picture.

Fill in the blanks with *next to, above, behind, in front of, below,* or *down*.

1. The teddy bear is _____ Lionel.

2. Lionel is _____ Jerome.

3. Tara is climbing _____ the stairs.

4. Jerome is _____ Lionel.

5. The cat is hiding _____ the teddy bear.

6. The teddy bear is _____ the cat.

Put on Your Thinking Cap!

Pauline has a few pots of flowers in her backyard.
Draw the flowers in each pot.

- The pot with 4 flowers is next to the pot with 2 flowers.
- The pot with 3 flowers is <u>not</u> fourth from the left.
- The pot with 2 flowers is first on the left.
- The pot with 1 flower is next to the pot with 3 flowers.

Numbers to 20

Lesson 1   Counting to 20

Write the numbers.

1.

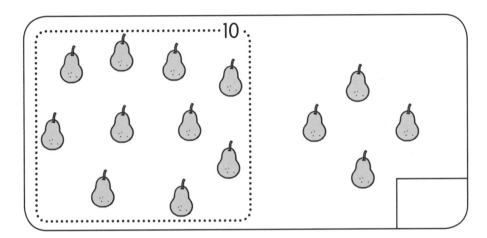

2.

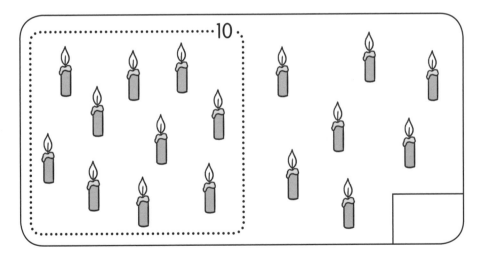

3.

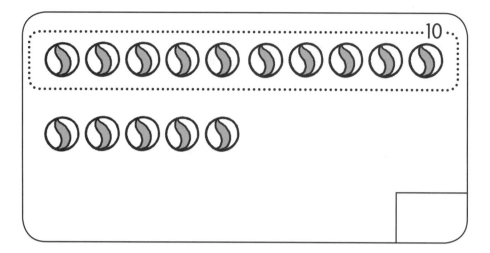

4.

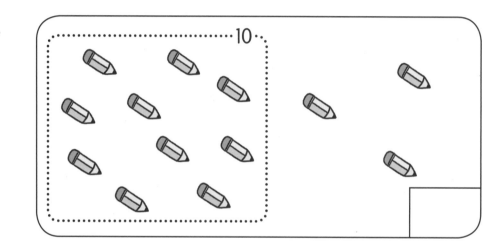

Count and write the number.

5.

_____

6.

_____

Name: _____ Date: _____

Match each number and word to the correct picture.

7. thirteen ● 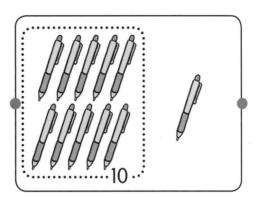 ● 15

8. twenty ● 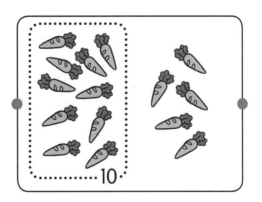 ● 11

9. eleven ● 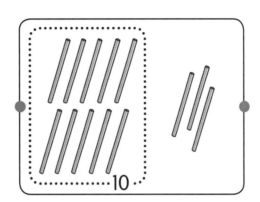 ● 13

10. fifteen ● 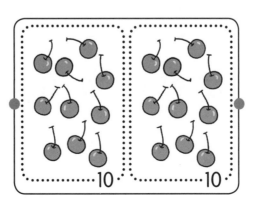 ● 20

Count.
Circle the correct number.

11.

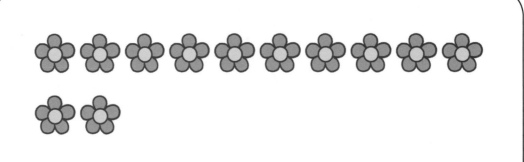

11   12   13

12.

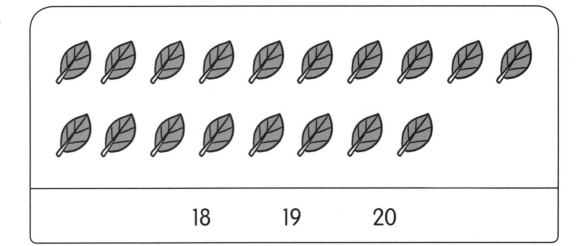

18   19   20

13.

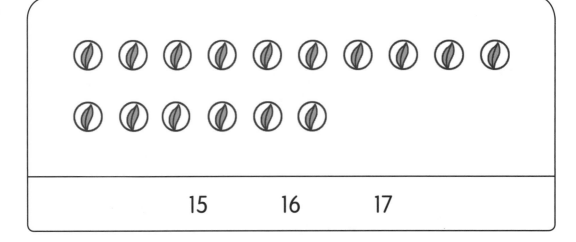

15   16   17

14.

| 12 | 13 | 14 |

15.

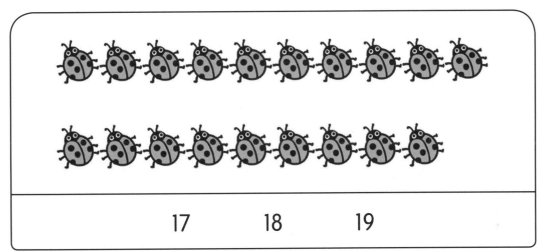

| 17 | 18 | 19 |

16.

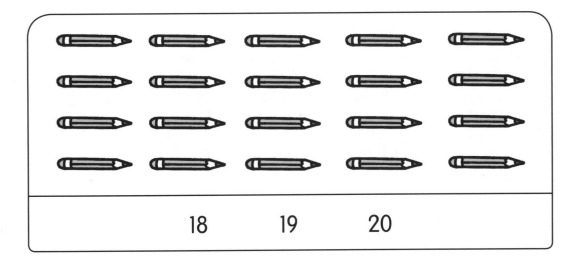

| 18 | 19 | 20 |

Circle to make a ten.
Fill in the blanks.

17.

10 and 6 make _____.

18.

_____ is 10 and 5.

19.

10 and 4 make _____.

20.

_____ and 10 make 13.

21.

10 and _____ make 10.

Lesson 2   Place Value

Look at the pictures.
Fill in the blanks.

1.

13 = _____ ten _____ ones

2.

16 = _____ ten _____ ones

3.

12 = _____ ten _____ ones

Fill in the place-value charts.

4.

18

Tens	Ones

5.

12

Tens	Ones

6.

20

Tens	Ones

7.

17

Tens	Ones

Fill in the blanks.

8.

Tens	Ones
1	0

_____

9.

Tens	Ones
2	8

_____

Count.

10.

Tens	Ones

_____

11.

Tens	Ones

_____

Lesson 3   Comparing Numbers

Count and compare.

1.

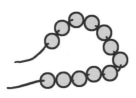

String A   **String B**

String _____ has more beads than String _____.

Circle the set that has more.

2.

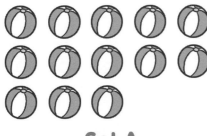

Set A   **Set B**

3.

Set A   **Set B**

Name: _____   Date: _____

Color the shirt that shows a number greater than 12 but less than 15.

4.

11   14   17   12

Fill in the blanks using these numbers.

15   13   18   17   16

5. _____ is less than 15.

6. _____ is greater than 17.

7. _____ is less than 18 but greater than 16.

Color the shape that shows the greatest number.

8.

16   13   14

9. 9   19   8

10.

11   17   16

Lesson 4 Making Patterns and Ordering Numbers

Fill in the blanks.

1. 3 more than 11 is _____.

2. 20 is 2 more than _____.

3. 2 less than 16 is _____.

4. 18 is 2 less than _____.

5. _____ is 2 less than 11.

6. _____ is 3 less than 16.

Fill in the blanks.

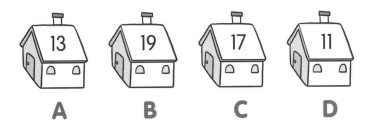

7. House _____ has the least number.

8. House _____ has the greatest number.

9. The number on House _____ is less than the number on House A.

Fill in the blanks using these numbers.

10. 13 is greater than _____.

11. 17 is greater than 15 but less than _____.

12. The least number is _____.

13. The greatest number is _____.

14. _____ is less than 17 but greater than 13.

15. _____ is greater than 12 but less than 15.

16. Order the numbers from least to greatest.

_____, _____, _____, _____, _____

least

© Marshall Cavendish International (Singapore) Private Limited.

● Order the numbers.

17. from greatest to least

(17)　　(20)　　(15)　　(11)

_____, _____, _____, _____

greatest

18. from least to greatest

[13]　　[11]　　[8]　　[19]

_____, _____, _____, _____

least

Complete each number pattern.

19.

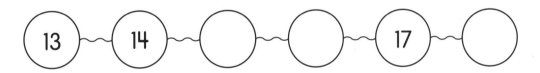

(13)—(14)—(○)—(○)—(17)—(○)

20.

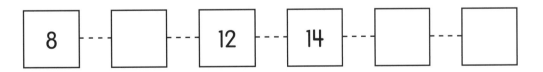

[8]--[ ]--[12]--[14]--[ ]--[ ]

21.

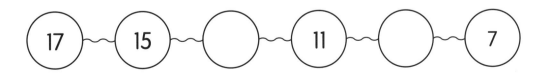

(17)—(15)—(○)—(11)—(○)—(7)

22.

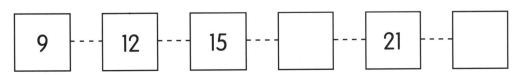

[9]--[12]--[15]--[ ]--[21]--[ ]

Name: ______________________ Date: ______________

Which number is missing from the pattern? Circle the missing number.

23. 18 16 ___?___ 12 10

13 or 14

24. 6 ___?___ 12 15 18

9 or 10

25. 4 8 12 ___?___ 20

15 or 16

 Put on Your Thinking Cap!

1.   Each shape stands for a number.

☆ and △ make 14.

◯ and ☆ make 11.

If ◯ and ◯ make 6,

then ◯ stands for _____,

△ stands for _____,

and ☆ stands for _____.

Complete the number bonds.

2.

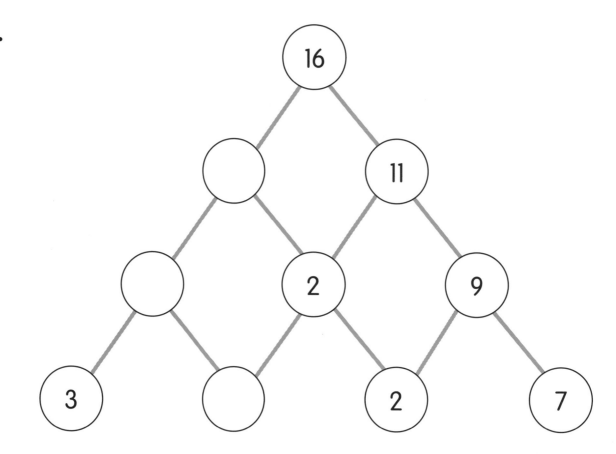

CHAPTER 8 Addition and Subtraction Facts to 20

Lesson 1   Ways to Add (Part 1)

Circle to make a 10.
Add.

1.

$5 + 6 =$ _____

2.

$9 + 7 =$ _____

Make a 10.
Then add.

3.

 $+$

$4 + 8 = 2 + 10$

$=$ _____

2   2

4.

$6 + 7 =$ _____ + _____

= _____

5.

$3 + 9 =$ _____ + _____

= _____

Make a 10.
Then add.

6.

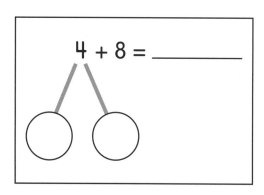

$4 + 8 =$ _____

7.

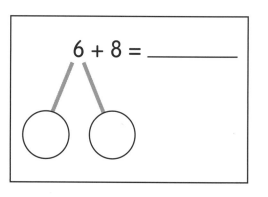

$6 + 8 =$ _____

Name: _____   **Date:** _____

Make a 10.
Then add.

8.

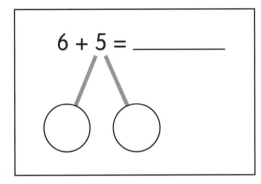

$6 + 5 =$ _____

9.

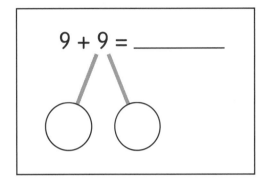

$9 + 9 =$ _____

Color the car that gives the least answer.

10.

8 + 9   6 + 7   9 + 5   7 + 8

Color the car that gives the greatest answer.

11.

7 + 5   9 + 7   5 + 9   8 + 2

Complete the addition sentences.

12.
☆ ☆ ☆ ☆ ☆ ☆ ☆
☆ ☆ ☆ ☆ ☆

$$7 + 6 = \text{_____}$$

13.
○ ○ ○ ○ ○ ○ ○ ○
○ ○ ○ ○

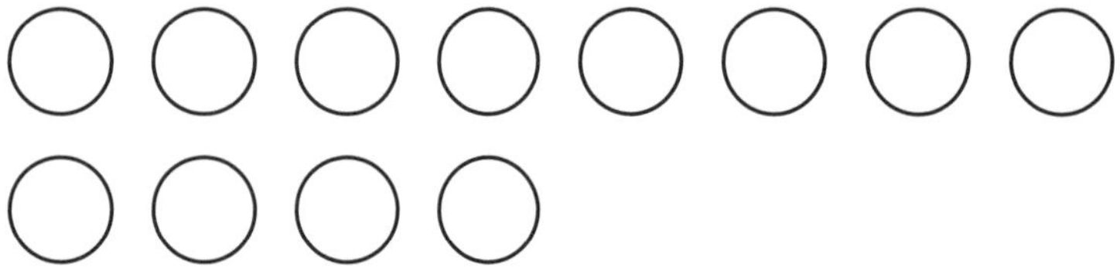

$$8 + 4 = \text{_____}$$

14.
△ △ △ △ △ △ △
△ △ △ △ △ △ △ △

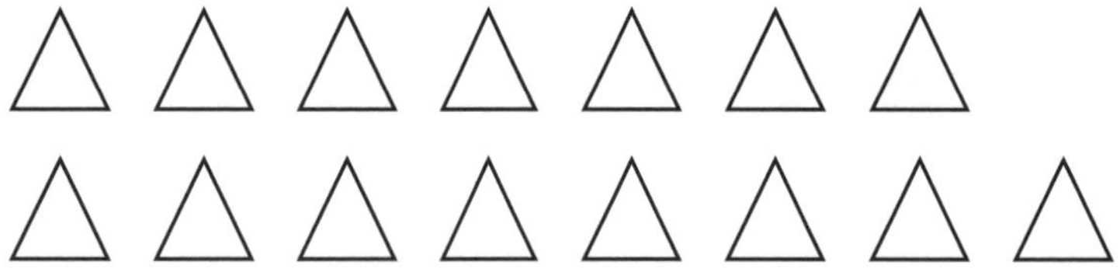

$$7 + 8 = \text{_____}$$

15.
☐ ☐ ☐ ☐ ☐ ☐ ☐ ☐ ☐
☐ ☐ ☐

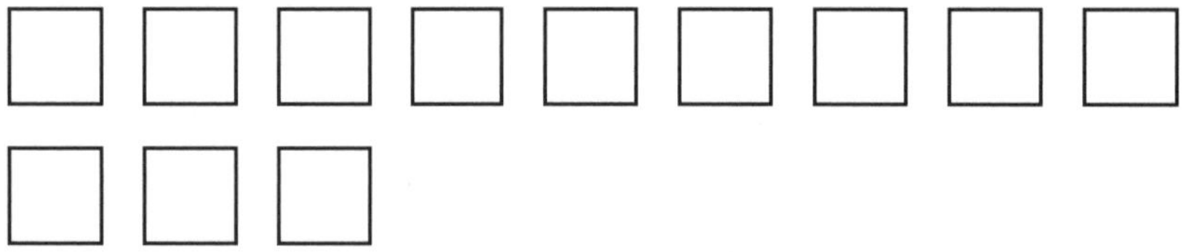

$$9 + 3 = \text{_____}$$

Lesson 1   Ways to Add (Part 2)

Group the number into a 10 and ones.
Then add.

1.

$17 + 2 =$ _____

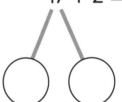

2.

$11 + 4 =$ _____

3.

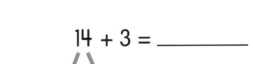

$14 + 3 =$ _____

4.

6 + 12 = _____

○   ○

5.   🧱 🧱 🧱   🧱 🧱 🧱 🧱 🧱 🧱 🧱 🧱 🧱 🧱 🧱

3 + 11 = _____

○   ○

Add.

6.   13 + 6 = _____   **7.**   15 + 3 = _____

8.   11 + 5 = _____   **9.**   3 + 13 = _____

10.   8 + 11 = _____   **11.**   12 + 5 = _____

Lesson 1   Ways to Add (Part 3)

Match.

1.

   ●   ●

2.

   ●   ●

3.

   ●   ●

4.

   ●   ●

5.

   ●   ●

6.

   ●   ●

Add the doubles plus one numbers.
Use doubles facts to help you.

7.   4 + 5 = _____

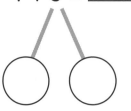

Doubles fact:

_____ + _____ = _____

8.   8 + 9 = _____

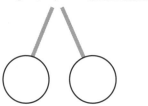

Doubles fact:

_____ + _____ = _____

9.   5 + 6 = _____

Doubles fact:

_____ + _____ = _____

10.   7 + 8 = _____

Doubles fact:

_____ + _____ = _____

11.   3 + 4 = _____

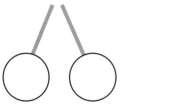

Doubles fact:

_____ + _____ = _____

12.   6 + 7 = _____

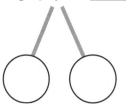

Doubles fact:

_____ + _____ = _____

Lesson 2 Ways to Subtract

Group the numbers into a 10 and ones.
Then subtract.

1.

$17 - 5 =$ _____

2.

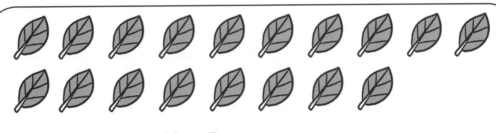

$15 - 3 =$ _____

3.

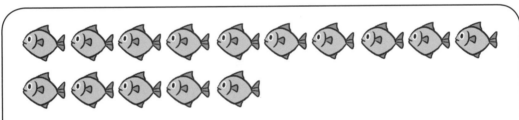

$18 - 5 =$ _____

4.

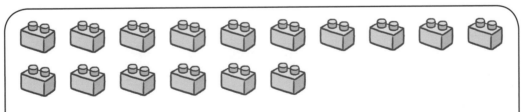

$16 - 5 =$ _____

Group the numbers into a 10 and ones.
Then subtract.

5.   16 – 6 = _____

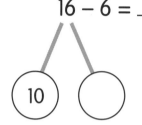

6.   13 – 2 = _____

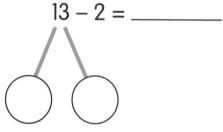

7.   14 – 3 = _____

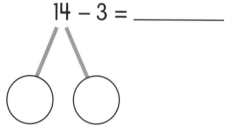

8.   17 – 5 = _____

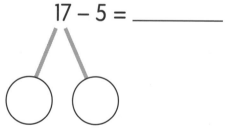

9.   20 – 6 = _____

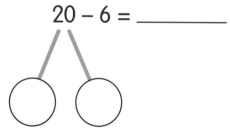

Group the numbers into a 10 and ones.
Then subtract.

┌─ **Example** ─────────────────────────────────┐

11 − 4 = ?   10 − 4 = 6

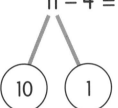   1 + 6 = 7

    (10)   (1)   So, 11 − 4 = 7.

└──┘

10.

15 − 7 = ?   _____ − _____ = _____

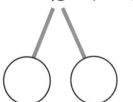   _____ + _____ = _____

   ( )   ( )   So, 15 − 7 = _____.

11.

13 − 4 = ?   _____ − _____ = _____

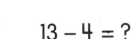   _____ + _____ = _____

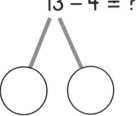   So, 13 − 4 = _____.

Name: _____   Date: _____

12.

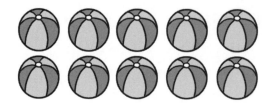

$12 - 6 = ?$

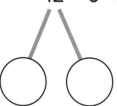

_____ − _____ = _____

_____ + _____ = _____

So, $12 - 6 =$ _____.

13.

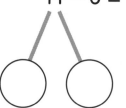

$14 - 6 = ?$

_____ − _____ = _____

_____ + _____ = _____

So, $14 - 6 =$ _____.

14.

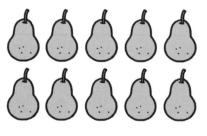 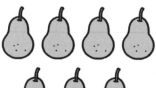 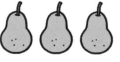

$17 - 8 = ?$

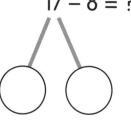

_____ − _____ = _____

_____ + _____ = _____

So, $17 - 8 =$ _____.

Use number bonds to subtract.

15.   20 – 6 = _____

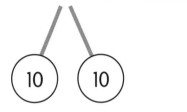

16.   18 – 6 = _____

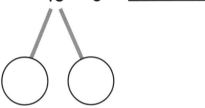

17.   15 – 9 = _____

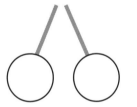

18.   12 – 9 = _____

19.   13 – 5 = _____

20. 15 – _____ = 10

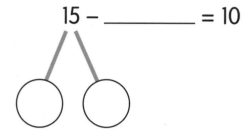

21. 16 – _____ = 13

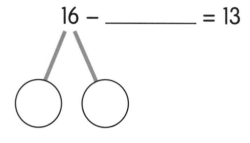

22. 14 – _____ = 8

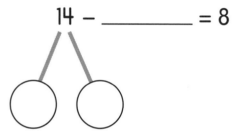

23. 11 – _____ = 5

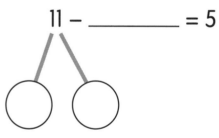

24. 17 – _____ = 9

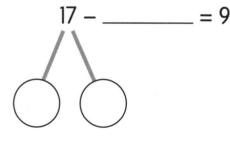

© Marshall Cavendish International (Singapore) Private Limited.

Lesson 3 Real-World Problems: Addition and Subtraction Facts

Solve.
Write a number sentence.

1. Mark collects 10 seashells.
    Ben collects 2 fewer seashells than Mark.
    How many seashells does Ben collect?

Ben collects _____ seashells.

2. 7 boys are playing.
    6 boys join them.
    How many boys are playing now?

There are _____ boys playing now.

3.   There are 16 apples.
4 of them are green.
How many apples are <u>not</u> green?

_____ apples are not green.

4.   Pamela has 12 beads.
Tina has 8 more beads than Pamela.
How many beads does Tina have?

Tina has _____ beads.

5.   Andrew caught some butterflies.
8 of them flew away.
He had 4 left.
How many butterflies did Andrew catch?

Andrew caught _____ butterflies.

 Put on Your Thinking Cap!

1.

Albert   **Jenny**   **May**

May has 10 fewer marbles than Albert.
May has 5 more marbles than Jenny.
Albert gives 4 marbles to Jenny.
May gives another 6 marbles to Jenny.
Jenny has 13 marbles now.

Find the number of marbles each of them had at first.

Jenny had _____ marbles.

May had _____ marbles.

Albert had _____ marbles.

2. Ben, Caleb, and Derek collect seashells at the beach.
Ben has 8 seashells.
Caleb has 10 more seashells than Ben but only
6 more than Derek.
How many seashells does each of them have?

Ben has _____ seashells.

Caleb has _____ seashells.

Derek has _____ seashells.

CHAPTER 9 Length

Lesson 1   Comparing Two Things

Circle the correct answer.

1. Which is longer?

2. Which is shorter?

3. Which is taller?

4. Which is shorter?

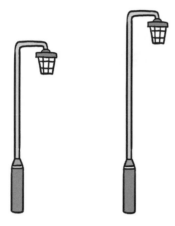

Draw.

5. a shorter brush

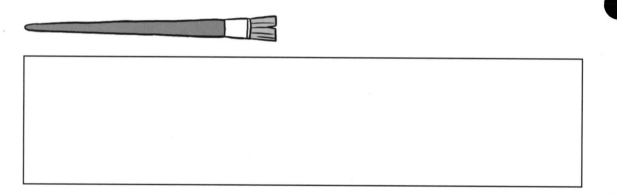

6. a taller tree

Lesson 2   Comparing More Than Two Things

Circle.

1.   the shortest object

2.   the longest object

3.   the tallest plant

Check (✓) the correct sentences.
Cross out (✗) the wrong sentences.

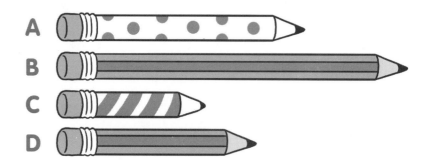

A
B
C
D

4. Pencil A is shorter than Pencil B. ☐

5. Pencil D is the shortest. ☐

6. Pencil B is the longest. ☐

Fill in the names of the boys.

8. _____

7. _____   9. _____

- Joe is taller than Dan.
- Bill is the shortest.

Fill in the blanks with *taller, tallest, shorter,* or *shortest.*

Papa Bear   Mama Bear   Baby Bear   Uncle Bear

10. Papa Bear is the _____.

11. Baby Bear is the _____.

12. Baby Bear is _____ than Uncle Bear.

13. Papa Bear is _____ than Mama Bear.

14. Mama Bear is _____ than Baby Bear

but _____ than Uncle Bear.

Compare.
Fill in the blanks.

Alice

Brenda

Colin

15. _____ is the tallest.

16. _____ is the shortest.

17. Brenda is taller than _____ but

shorter than _____.

Match.

18.

| tallest | shortest |

Lesson 3   Using a Start Line

Compare.
Fill in the blanks.

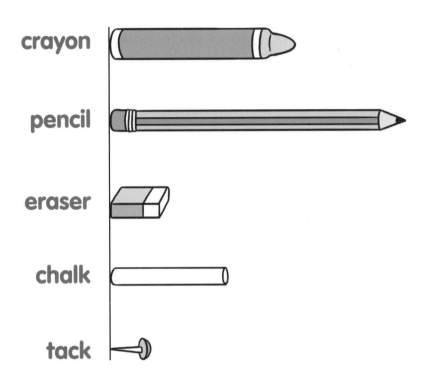

crayon

pencil

eraser

chalk

tack

1.   The _____ is the shortest.

2.   The _____ is the longest.

3.   The crayon is shorter than the _____.

4.   The eraser is longer than the _____.

Name: _____   Date: _____

5.   Order the things from shortest to longest.

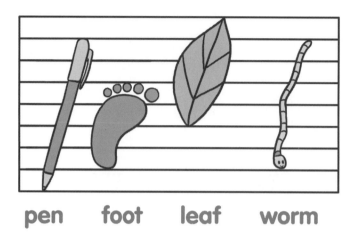

pen   foot   leaf   worm

_____, _____, _____, _____

shortest

6.   Order the things from longest to shortest.

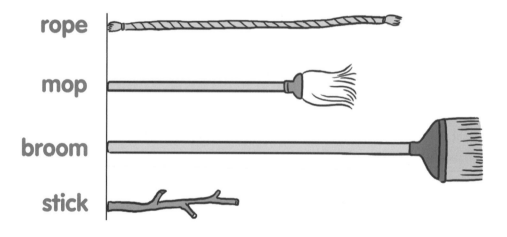

rope

mop

broom

stick

_____, _____, _____, _____

longest

Lesson 4 Measuring Things

Look at the picture.
Fill in the blanks.

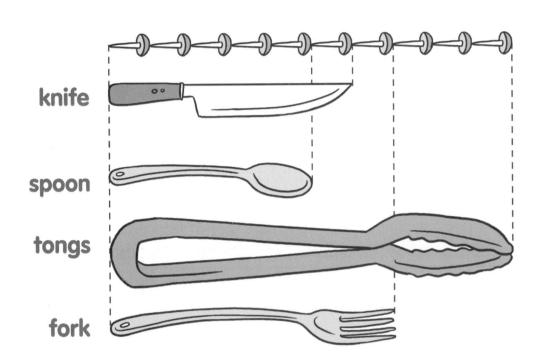

knife

spoon

tongs

fork

1. The knife is about _____ long.

2. The spoon is about _____ long.

3. The pair of tongs is about _____ long.

4. The fork is shorter than the _____.

5. The _____ is longer than the

_____ but shorter than the fork.

6. The _____ is the shortest.

Look at the picture.
Fill in the blanks.

7.

The toy train is about _____ 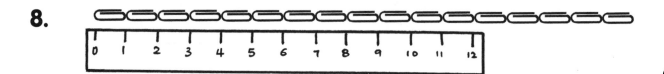 long.

8.

The ruler is about _____ ⬭ long.

9.

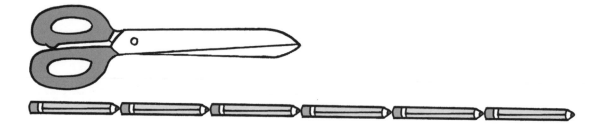

The scissors are about _____ ✏ long.

Lesson 5   Finding Length in Units

Look at the picture.
Fill in the blanks.

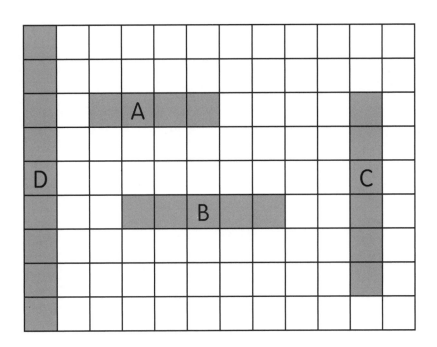

Each ☐ stands for 1 unit.

1.   Rectangle A is _____ units long.

2.   Rectangle _____ is the longest.

3.   Rectangle C is longer than Rectangles _____

     and _____ .

Look at the picture.
Fill in the blanks.
Each ☐ stands for 1 unit.

4. The ⬜ is about _____ units long.

5. The 🐛 is about _____ units long.

6. Each 🌷 is about _____ units tall.

7. The 🌻 is about _____ units tall.

8. The 👧 is about _____ units tall.

9. The 🐶 is about _____ units tall.

Circle.

10. The (🐶 / 👧 / 🌻) is the tallest.

11. The (⬜ / 🐛) is longer.

Look at the picture.
Fill in the blanks.

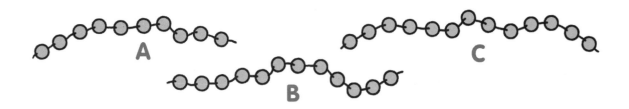

Each ⊘ stands for 1 unit.

12.   Bracelet _____ is the longest.

13.   Bracelet C is _____ units long.

14.   Bracelet A is _____ units long.

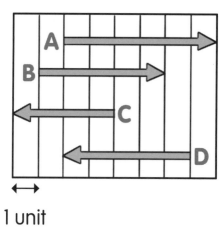

1 unit

15.   How long is Arrow A? _____ units

16.   Which is the shortest arrow? Arrow _____

Look at the picture.
Fill in the blanks.

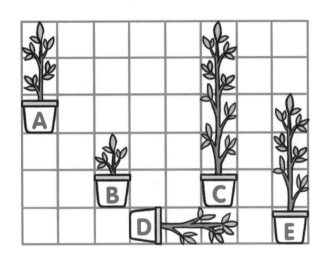

Each ▢ stands for 1 unit.

17. Plant _____ is the shortest. It is _____ units tall.

18. Plant _____ and Plant _____ are of the same height.

19. Plant _____ is the tallest.

20. Which plant is 4 units tall? Plant _____.

Look at the picture.
Fill in the blanks.

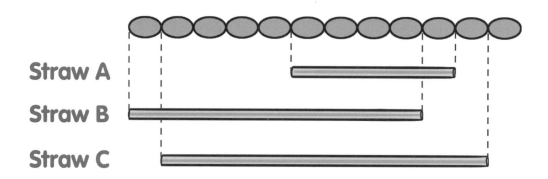

1 ⬭ is 1 unit.

21. Straw A is about _____ units long.

22. Straw B is about _____ units long.

23. Straw C is about _____ units long.

24. Straw _____ is the shortest.

25. Straw _____ is the longest.

26. Straw B is longer than Straw _____ but shorter

than Straw _____.

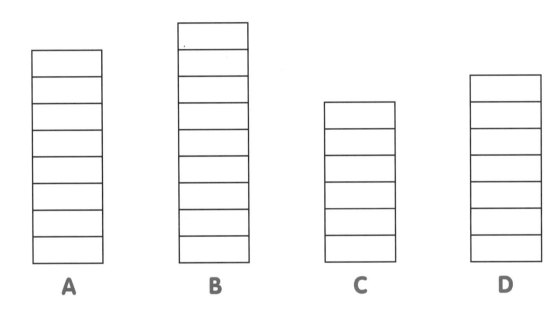

Put on Your Thinking Cap!

Ron, Trent, Sally, and Mandy each made a tower using toy blocks.

A   B   C   D

- Ron's tower is taller than Mandy's tower.
- Mandy's tower is the shortest.
- Sally's tower is shorter than Ron's tower.
- Trent's tower is shorter than Sally's tower.

1.   Name the tower that each child made.

Ron: Tower _____   Sally: Tower _____

Trent: Tower _____   Mandy: Tower _____

2.   A sandwich is about 5 units long.

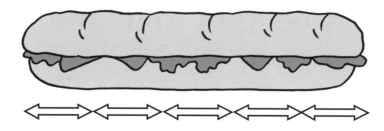

1 ⟺ stands for 1 unit.

The length of 3 sandwiches like this one is about

_____ units long.

Name: _____ Date: _____

Mid-Year Test Prep

Multiple Choice (20 × 2 points = 40 points)

Fill in the circle next to the correct answer.

1. How many bees are there?

    (A) 5   (B) 6   (C) 7   (D) 8

2. Thirteen comes just before _____.

    (A) fifteen

    (B) fourteen

    (C) twelve

    (D) twenty

3. _____ + 3 = 1 ten 3 ones

    (A) 1   (B) 10   (C) 11   (D) 13

4. Which animal is 4th from the right?

crab   seahorse   goldfish   octopus

(A) crab

(B) goldfish

(C) octopus

(D) seahorse

5. Complete the pattern.

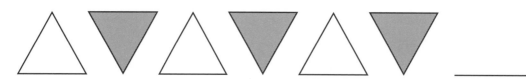

(A)

(B)

(C)

(D)

6. Which two numbers make 16?

Ⓐ

Ⓑ

Ⓒ

Ⓓ 9 6

7. There are _____ triangles in the picture.

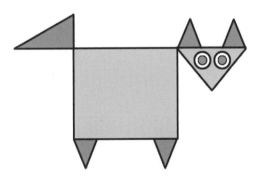

Ⓐ 4   Ⓑ 5   Ⓒ 6   Ⓓ 8

8. Complete the number pattern.

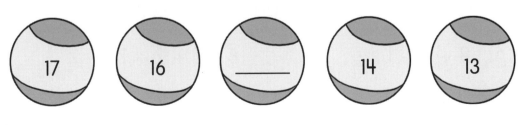

Ⓐ 6   Ⓑ 10   Ⓒ 12   Ⓓ 15

9. 2 less than 14 is _____.

    (A) 10   (B) 11   (C) 12   (D) 16

10. 7 + 5 is the same as _____.

    (A) 6 + 4   (B) 7 + 2

    (C) 8 + 5   (D) 10 + 2

11. _____ less than 13 is 8.

    (A) 4   (B) 5   (C) 6   (D) 18

12. 1 ten 2 ones + 3 ones = _____.

    (A) 1 ten 5 ones

    (B) 16

    (C) 2 tens

    (D) 15 tens

13. 9 – 3 is equal to 3 + _____.

    (A) 3   (B) 5   (C) 6   (D) 12

14. Which of these shows a doubles-plus one fact?

    (A) 2 + 4 + 1   (B) 2 + 2 + 1

    (C) 11 + 1   (D) 2 + 2 + 2

15. Which caterpillar is the longest?

Ⓐ A   Ⓑ B   Ⓒ C   Ⓓ D

16. Complete the number bond.

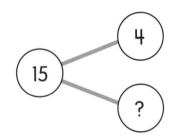

Ⓐ 9   Ⓑ 10   Ⓒ 11   Ⓓ 19

17. The straw is about _____ ⬯ long.

Ⓐ 10   Ⓑ 11   Ⓒ 14   Ⓓ 18

18. The shaded shape is a _____.

Ⓐ square

Ⓒ circle

Ⓑ triangle

Ⓓ rectangle

19. Which shape can you stack, slide, and roll?

Ⓐ rectangular prism

Ⓑ cylinder

Ⓒ circle

Ⓓ rectangle

20. The numbers in the 4th and 8th shapes add up to _____.

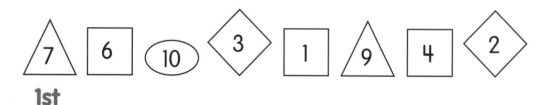

1st

Ⓐ 5   Ⓑ 6   Ⓒ 10   Ⓓ 17

Name: _____   **Date:** _____

Short Answer

Order the numbers from greatest to least. (2 points)

21.

_____   _____   _____   _____

greatest

Color the set that gives the least answer. (1 point)

22.   (6 + 9)   (10 + 8)   (11 + 2)   (12 + 4)

Fill in the blanks. (2 points)

23.   12 + _____ = 20

24.   _____ – 7 = 3

Write + or – in the circle. (1 point)

25.   11 ◯ 7 = 18

Look at the picture.
Fill in the blanks. (3 points)

Kate   Deon   Lola   Sue   Tom

26. Who is 1st in the race? _____

27. Who is behind Lola in the race? _____

28. Who is Sue in front of? _____

Circle. (1 point)

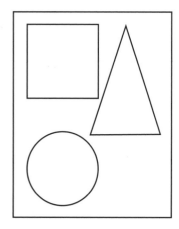 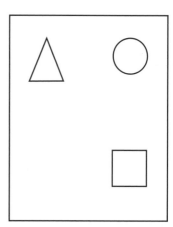 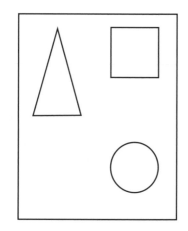

29. The shapes are sorted by (size / shape).

● **Circle the tallest animal.** (1 point)

30.

● **Look at the picture.**
Fill in the blank. (2 points)

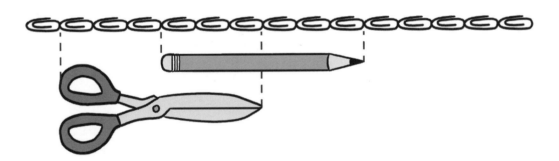

31. The length of the pencil and the pair of scissors is

about _____ ⊂ in all.

Complete the pattern.
Color the shape that comes next. (2 points)

32.

Look at the picture.
Write two number sentences. (4 points)

33. _____ + _____ = _____

34. _____ − _____ = _____

Fill in the blank. (2 points)

35.

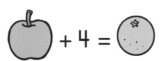

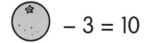

Extended Response (5 × 4 points = 20 points)

Solve.

36. Anna has 8 stickers.
Belle has 6 stickers.
How many stickers do they have in all?

They have _____ stickers in all.

37. Joel has 15 pets.
5 of them are birds.
The rest are rabbits.
How many pet rabbits does Joel have?

Joel has _____ pet rabbits.

38. Mike has 12 toy cars.
Ned has 4 toy cars more than Mike.
How many toy cars does Ned have?

Ned has _____ toy cars.

39. David had 20 coins.
He gave some coins to Peter.
David had 8 coins left.
How many coins did David give to Peter?

David gave _____ coins to Peter.

40. Rope A is longer than Rope C
but shorter than Rope B.
Rope D is shorter than Rope C.

   a. Which rope is the shortest?

      Rope _____

   b. Which rope is the longest?

      Rope _____

Answers

Chapter 1

Lesson 1

1. 5   2. 3

3.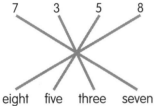

4. ⭐ ⭐   ⭐ ☆

   ⭐ ⭐   ☆ ☆

5. four   6. eight

7. six

8. 7   3   5   8

   eight   five   three   seven

9. 5   10. 3

11. 0   12. 8

13. 1   14. two

15. four   16. one

17. two   18. six/6

19. 0, <u>1</u>, 2, <u>3</u>, 4, 5   20. 10, <u>9</u>, <u>8</u>, 7, 6

21. 5, <u>6</u>, 7, 8, <u>9</u>, 10   22. 6, 5, <u>4</u>, <u>3</u>, 2

23.

🦆	(two)	one	four	six
🦘	three	six	(four)	five
🦒	(five)	seven	nine	six
🐻	one	(three)	two	ten

Lesson 2

1. igloos, people

2. fewer

3. more

4.

5.

6.

7.

8. 2

9.

10.

11.

12.

13.   4   14.   1

15.   7   16.   5

17.   9   18.   10

19.   5   20.   7

21.

22.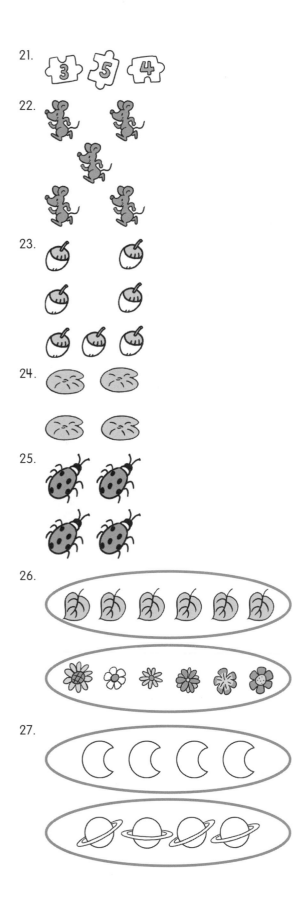

23.

24.

25.

26.

27.

Lesson 3

1.

2.

3.

4. bird, nest

5. leaf, caterpillar

6. C

7. A

8. D

9. 6, 5, 4, 3, <u>2</u>, <u>1</u>

10. 8, 7, <u>6</u>, <u>5</u>, 4, 3

11. 0, 1, <u>2</u>, 3, <u>4</u>

12. 5, <u>6</u>, 7, <u>8</u>, 9, 10

13. 8, <u>7</u>, <u>6</u>, 5, 4

14. 8

15. 7

16. 9

17. 6

18. 5

19. 9

20. 1

Put on Your Thinking Cap!

1–2. Thinking Skill: Spatial Visualization

Solution:

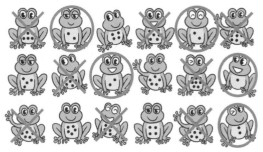

3. Thinking Skill: Problem Solving

Strategy: Make a systematic list

Solution:

__ + __ = 5

4 + 1 = 5

3 + 2 = 5

Look at the parts of the whole.

Which part is 1 more than the other?

Jake has 3 bones and Ginger has 2 bones.

Chapter 2

Lesson 1 (Part 1)

1. 3, 5

2. 2

3. 0

4. 1

5. 1

6. 4

7. 2

8. 6

9.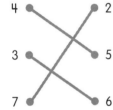

10. (8)—(10)—(2)

11. 3, 2
    4, 1
    0, 5 Accept all answers.

12. 1, 6
    2, 5
    3, 4
    0, 7 Accept any two answers.

13. 1, 5
    2, 4
    3, 3
    0, 6 Accept any three answers.

Lesson 1 (Part 2)

1. 8, 2

2. 7, 1

3. 5, 4

4. 0, 6

5.
    4 • ╲ ╱ • 2
    3 • ╳ • 5
    7 • ╱ ╲ • 6

6. 8 • ╲ ╱ • 1
    9 • ╱ ╲ • 2

    3 •———• 7

7.

8. 7

9. 2

Lesson 1 (Part 3)

1. 5

2. 3, 1 or 1, 3

3. 7

4. 1, 2 or 2, 1

5. 3

6. 8

7.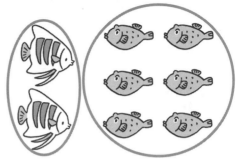

8.

9.
    (3)—(4)—(1)

10.
    (2)—(4)—(2)

11.
    (7)—(2)—(1)(2)(4)

12.
    (9)—(3)—(2)(3)(4)

13.
    (6)—(2)—(1)(2)(3)

Put on Your Thinking Cap!

Thinking Skill: Analyzing Parts and Whole

Solution:

1.

7 (2)—(9)—(7)

2.

Chapter 3

Lesson 1 (Part 1)
1. $4 + 2 = 6$
2. $4 + 6 = 10$
3. $2 + 7 = 9$
4. 9
5. 9
6. 10
7. 9
8. 8
9. 7
10. 7, ⑩, 8, 8
11. 7
12. 10
13. 5
14. 7

Lesson 1 (Part 2)
1. 6 (5, 6, 1)
2. $3 + 3 = 6$ (3, 6, 3)
3. $5 + 2 = 7$ (5, 7, 2)
4. $5 + 3 = 8$ (5, 8, 3)
5. $7 + 2 = 9$ (7, 9, 2)
6. $4 + 1 = 5$ (4, 5, 1)
7. 9 (6, 9, 3)
8. 7 (2, 7, 5)
9. 4 (3, 7, 4)
10. 0 (0, 8, 8)
11. 2 (4, 6, 2)

12.

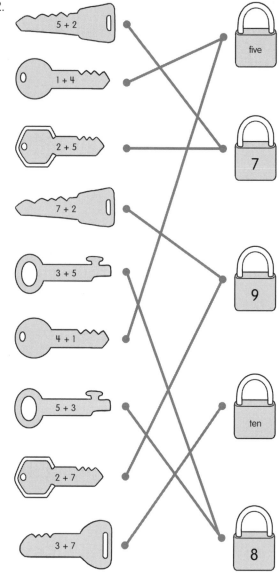

Lesson 2
1. 4
   2
   $4 + 2 = 6$
   6
2. Answers vary.
3. Answers vary.
4. 3
5. 7, 9

Lesson 3
1. $6 + 3 = 9$
   9
2. 7
   2
   $7 + 2 = 9$
   9

3. 3
   4
   3 + 4 = 7
   7
4. 2
   3
   2 + 3 = 5
   5

Put on Your Thinking Cap!

1. Thinking Skill: Logical Reasoning

   Solution:
   Red
   Green
   Yellow
   Blue

2. Thinking Skill: Guess and Check

   Solution:

Chapter 4

Lesson 1 (Part 1)

1.

   3

2.

   5

3.

   1

4.	3	5.	5	6.	1	7.	3
8.	2	9.	5	10.	7	11.	4
12.	8	13.	5	14.	5	15.	1
16.	2	17.	2	18.	5	19.	6
20.	2	21.	7	22.	4	23.	4
24.	6	25.	1	26.	2		

Lesson 1 (Part 2)

1. 4

2. 5

3. 4   4. 1

5. 8 − 1 = _7_

6. 10 − 5 = _5_

7. 6 − 0 = _6_

8. 9 − 6 = _3_

9. 10 − 6 = _4_

10. 4 − 4 = _0_

11.	8	12.	5	13.	4	14.	3

15. 9 − _6_ = _3_, 3   16. _5_ − 3 = _2_, 2

Lesson 2

1. 2, 7 − _2_ = _5_, 5   2. 5, 4, _5_ − _4_ = _1_, 1

3. 8, 3, 8 − 3 = 5, 5   4. 5, 2, 5 − 2 = 3, 3

Lesson 3

1. 9 − 3 = 6, 6   2. 7 − 3 = 4, 4
3. 6 − 1 = 5, 5   4. 8 − 3 = 5, 5
5. 5 − 3 = 2, 2   6. 9 − 2 = 7, 7
7. 7 − 2 = 5, 5

Lesson 4

1. 6 + 2 = 8   2. 3 + 1 = 4
   2 + 6 = 8   1 + 3 = 4
   8 − 2 = 6   4 − 3 = 1
   8 − 6 = 2   4 − 1 = 3
3. 7   4. 4

Extra Practice 1A   **169**

Put on Your Thinking Cap!

Thinking Skill: Induction and Deduction

Solution:

1. 6
2. 8
3. 4
4. 10
5. Thinking Skill: Analyzing Parts and Whole

   Strategy: Guess and Check

   Solution:

   There are two possible answers.

   2 cats and 1 parrot or 1 cat and 3 parrots.

   Since Peter has 4 pets, he has 1 cat and 3 parrots.

Test Prep for Chapters 1 to 4

1. C
2. D
3. D
4. B
5. C
6. B
7. A
8. B
9. C
10. A
11. carrots, rabbits
12. –
13. +
14–17.

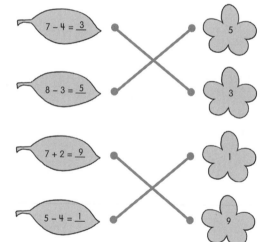

18. 8
19. 9
20. 1
21. 2
22. 4 + 4, 5 + 3
23. 8 – 2 = 6
24. 5 + 3 = 8
25. 3 + 5 = 8
26. 8 – 3 = 5
27. 8 – 5 = 3
28. 10
29. 0
30. 3
31. 3
32. 8
33. 6 + 2 = 8, 8
34. 10 – 4 = 6, 6

170   Answers

Chapter 5

Lesson 1 (Part 1)

1. circle
2. square
3. rectangle
4. triangle
5.

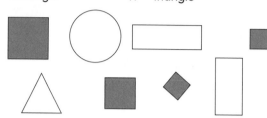

6.

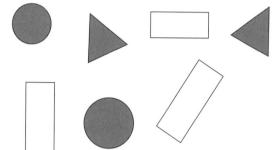

7. circle
8. circle
9.

10.

11.

12.

13. Answers vary.

Lesson 1 (Part 2)

1. squares: red
2. circles: blue
3. rectangles: green
4. triangles: yellow

Accept squares colored in green.

5. triangle
6. circle
7. square or rectangle

Lesson 2

1–6.

cylinder

sphere

cube

pyramid

rectangular prism

cone

7.

8. stack
9. slide
10. roll

Lesson 3 (Part 1)

1. 10
2. 6
3. 5
4. 2
5. triangles: green
6. 5
7. rectangles: blue
8. 6

9.

2

5

2

1

10.
5

2

3

2

11–14.
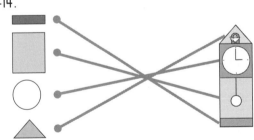

Lesson 3 (Part 2)

1.

E

A

B

D

C

2. Answers vary

Lesson 4

1. square
2. triangle
3. rectangle
4. circle
5. square
6. circle

7.
8.
9.
10.
11.

Lesson 5

1.
2.
3.
4. Answers vary
5. Answers vary
6. Answers vary

Lesson 6

1.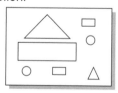
2.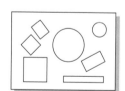
3.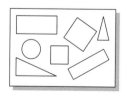
4.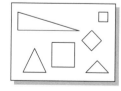

Put on Your Thinking Cap!

Thinking Skill: Spatial Visualization

Solution:

1.

Dana   Bob

Ally   Carl

Chapter 6

Lesson 1

1.
2.
3.
4.
5.
   1st
6.
   2nd
7.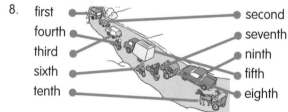
   3rd

8. first   second
   fourth   seventh
   third   ninth
   sixth   fifth
   tenth   eighth

9. C
10. D
11. D

Lesson 2 (Part 1)

1.
2.
3.
4.

5. 10
6. horse
7. seal
8. 3rd
9. 7th
10. horse
11. cat
12. horse
13. elephant
14. camel
15. tiger
16. monkey
17. third
18. first
19. triangle
20. square
21. last

Lesson 2 (Part 2)
1. next to
2. below
3. down
4. above
5. behind
6. in front of

Put on Your Thinking Cap!
Thinking Skill: Comparing
Solution: 2 flowers, 4 flowers, 3 flowers, 1 flower

Chapter 7

Lesson 1
1. 14
2. 17
3. 15
4. 13
5. 12
6. 17

7–10.

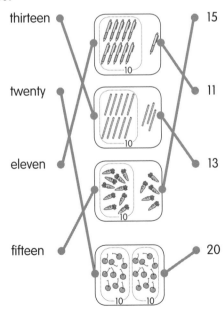

11. 12
12. 18
13. 16
14. 14
15. 19
16. 20
17. 16

18. 15
19. 14
20. 3
21. 0

Lesson 2
1. 1 ten 3 ones
2. 1 ten 6 ones
3. 1 ten 2 ones
4.

18	Tens	Ones
	1	8

5.

12	Tens	Ones
	1	2

6.

20	Tens	Ones
	2	0

7.

17	Tens	Ones
	1	7

8. 10
9. 28
10. 15
11. 19

Lesson 3
1. B, A
2. Set B
3. Set B
4. 14
5. 13
6. 18
7. 17
8. 16
9. 19
10. 17

Lesson 4
1. 14
2. 18
3. 14
4. 20
5. 9
6. 13
7. D
8. B
9. D
10. 12
11. 19
12. 12
13. 19
14. 15
15. 13
16. 12, 13, 15, 17, 19
17. 20, 17, 15, 11
18. 8, 11, 13, 19
19. 15, 16, 18
20. 10, 16, 18
21. 13, 9
22. 18, 24
23. 14
24. 9
25. 16

Put on Your Thinking Cap!

1. Thinking Skill: Solve Part of the Problem

   $\bigcirc = 3$, $\triangle = 6$, $\stackrel{\star}{} = 8$

2. Thinking Skill: Analyzing Parts and Whole

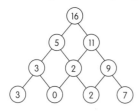

Chapter 8

Lesson 1 (Part 1)

1. 11

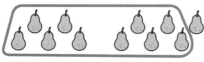

2. 16

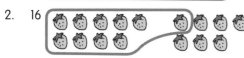

3. 12

4. $3 + 10 = 13$ ⑥ / ③ ③

5. $2 + 10 = 12$ ③ / ② ①

6. 12   ④ / ② ②

7. 14   ⑥ / ④ ②

8. 11   ⑤ / ④ ①

9. 18   ⑨ / ① ⑧

10. $6 + 7$

11. $9 + 7$

12. 13

13. 12

14. 15

15. 12

Lesson 1 (Part 2)

1. 19   ⑰ / ⑨ ⑧

2. 15   ⑪ / ⑤ ⑥

3. 17   ⑭ / ⑦ ⑦

4. 18   ⑫ / ④ ⑧

5. 14   ⑪ / ⑦ ④

6. 19   7. 18   8. 16   9. 16

10. 19   11. 17

Lesson 1 (Part 3)

1–6.

7. $9, 4 + 4 = 8$

8. $17, 8 + 8 = 16$

9. $11, 5 + 5 = 10$

10. $15, 7 + 7 = 14$

11. $7, 3 + 3 = 6$

12. $13, 6 + 6 = 12$

Lesson 2

1. 12   2. 12   3. 13   4. 11

5. 10   ⑯ / ⑩ ⑥

6. 11   ⑬ / ⑩ ③

7. 11   ⑭ / ⑩ ④

8. 12   ⑰ / ⑩ ⑦

9. 14   ⑳ / ⑩ ⑩

10.

   ⑮ / ⑩ ⑤ $10 - 7 = 3, 3 + 5 = 8, 8$

11.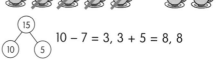

   ⑬ / ⑩ ③ $10 - 4 = 6, 6 + 3 = 9, 9$

12.

 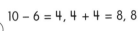

 10 − 6 = 4, 4 + 2 = 6, 6

13.

 10 − 6 = 4, 4 + 4 = 8, 8

14.

17 10 − 8 = 2, 2 + 7 = 9, 9
10 7

15. 14   16. 12   18
                           10   8

17. 6   15   18. 3   12
       10   5   10   2

19. 8   13   20. 5   15
       10   3   10   5

21. 3   16   22. 6   14
       10   6   10   4

23. 6   11   24. 8   17
       10   1   10   7

Lesson 3
1. 10 − 2 = 8, 8   2. 7 + 6 = 13, 13
3. 16 − 4 = 12, 12   4. 8 + 12 = 20, 20
5. 8 + 4 = 12, 12

Put on Your Thinking Cap!
1. Strategy: Work Backwards
   Solution:
   13 − 6 = 7
   7 − 4 = 3
   Jenny had 3 marbles.

   3 + 5 = 8
   May had 8 marbles.

   8 + 10 = 18
   Albert had 18 marbles.

2. Thinking Skill: Induction and Deduction
   Solution:
   Ben has 8 seashells.
   8 + 10 = 18
   Caleb has <u>18</u> seashells.
   18 − 6 = 12
   Derek has <u>12</u> seashells.

Chapter 9

Lesson 1
1.

2.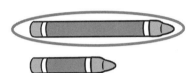

3.

4.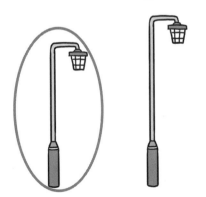

5. Answers vary   6. Answer vary

Lesson 2
1.

2.

3.

4. Pencil A is shorter than Pencil B. ✓

5. Pencil D is the shortest. ✗

6. Pencil B is the longest. ✓

7. Bill
8. Dan
9. Joe
10. tallest
11. shortest
12. shorter
13. taller
14. taller, shorter
15. Colin
16. Alice
17. Alice, Colin

18.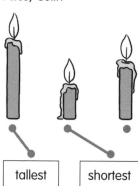

tallest	shortest

Lesson 3
1. tack
2. pencil
3. pencil
4. tack
5. foot, leaf, worm, pen
6. broom, rope, mop, stick

Lesson 4
1. 6
2. 5
3. 2
4. tongs
5. knife, spoon
6. spoon
7. 5
8. 12
9. 3

Lesson 5
1. 4
2. D
3. A, B
4. 16
5. 1
6. 2
7. 3
8. 9
9. 6

10.
11.

12. C
13. 13
14. 10
15. 6
16. C
17. B, 2
18. A, D
19. C
20. Plant E
21. 5
22. 9
23. 10
24. A
25. C
26. A, C

Put on Your Thinking Cap!
1. Thinking Skill: Comparing
   Solution:
   Ron: Tower B   Sally: Tower A
   Trent: Tower D   Mandy: Tower C
2. Thinking Skill: Spatial Visualization
   Solution:
   5 + 5 + 5 = 15
   15 units

Mid-Year Test Prep

1. C
2. B
3. B
4. A
5. D
6. B
7. C
8. D
9. C
10. D
11. B
12. A
13. A
14. B
15. C
16. C
17. B
18. C
19. B
20. A
21. 25, 12, 8, 6
22. 11 + 2
23. 8
24. 10
25. +
26. Kate
27. Sue
28. Tom
29. size
30.
31. 12
32.
33. 3 + 6 = 9 / 6 + 3 = 9
34. 9 − 3 = 6 / 9 − 6 = 3
35. 9
36. 8 + 6 = 14, 14
37. 15 − 5 = 10, 10
38. 12 + 4 = 16, 16
39. 20 − 8 = 12, 12
40. a. D   b. B